CARL NIELSEN STUDIES

VOLUME III   2008

DET
KGL

BIB
LIO
TEK

CARL NIELSEN STUDIES

VOLUME III   2008

Edited by David Fanning, Daniel Grimley, and Niels Krabbe (editor-in-chief)

Copenhagen 2008
The Royal Library

Graphic design Kontrapunkt A/S, Copenhagen

Text set in Swift

Printed by Quickly Tryk A/S, Copenhagen

ISSN 1603-3663

Sponsored by Forskningsrådet for Kultur og Kommunikation

Address Carl Nielsen Studies, The Royal Library
P.O. Box 2149, DK-1016 Copenhagen K, Denmark

Distribution This volume is distributed outside Scandinavia by Ashgate Publishing Limited,
Gower House, Croft Road, Aldershot, Hampshire, GU11 3HR, United Kingdom
Ashgate ISBN 978-0-7546-6558-8

CONTENTS

In the footnotes English translations for Danish titles of books and articles are given in brackets apart from the following, frequently quoted, books:

Torben Meyer & Frede Schandorf Petersen, *Carl Nielsen, Kunstneren og Mennesket* [Carl Nielsen, the Artist and the Man], Copenhagen 1948, 2 vols.

Irmelin Eggert Møller & Torben Meyer, *Carl Nielsens Breve: i udvalg og med kommentarer* [The Letters of Carl Nielsen: an annotated selection], Copenhagen 1954.

Torben Schousboe (ed.), *Carl Nielsen. Dagbøger og brevveksling med Anne Marie Carl-Nielsen* [Carl Nielsen. Diaries and Correspondence with Anne Marie Carl-Nielsen], Copenhagen 1983, 2 vols.

John Fellow (ed.), *Carl Nielsen til sin samtid* [Carl Nielsen to His Contemporaries], Copenhagen 1999, 3 vols.

John Fellow (ed.), *Carl Nielsen. Brevudgaven* [The Letters of Carl Nielsen], Copenhagen 2005- .

EDITORIAL

By Niels Krabbe

With this third volume of *Carl Nielsen Studies*, the publication enters the domain of peer review journals. The articles in this volume have all been accepted by a Danish or overseas scholar with expertise in the appropriate field. Four of the articles have been previously published, three of them in a Festschrift for Niels Krabbe, *Musikvidenskabelige Kompositioner. Festskrift til Niels Krabbe* in autumn 2006 (Fanning, Fellow, and Ahlgren Jensen, the first in a slightly revised version), while the fourth (Mathiassen) appeared as a chapter in his book, *Livet. musiken og samfundet. En bog om Carl Nielsen* (Life, Music, and Society: a book about Carl Nielsen) from 1986.[1] The fifth article (Vestergaard and Vorre) builds upon the authors' masters thesis from Aalborg University in 2005.

All of the articles represent an important contribution to Nielsen research in their own manner. Ahlgren Jensen examines the wider political contexts of the so-called "Rosenhoff-affair". The article reveals how, through analysis of the issue's press coverage, a political-educational agenda lay behind the dismissal of Nielsen's teacher and mentor at the conservatory, Orla Rosenhoff. Fellow undertakes an analysis of the reception history of one of Denmark's most popular patriotic songs, *Du danske Mand*, and reveals how its genesis and subsequent use stand in sharp opposition to each other. Fanning's article demonstrates the range of expression in Nielsen's First Symphony while simultaneously revealing the series of musical building blocks from other composers that can be found in the work, without necessarily implying that Nielsen was conscious of all of these musical references. Mathiassen focuses on Nielsen's relationship with a range of fundamental philosophical questions as he considers the oft-discussed subject of Nielsen's ambiguous attitude towards programme music. Finally, Vorre and Vestergaard discuss to what extent the myth of 'the national' in Nielsen's songs is a pure construction, or whether it is possible to identify something national within the musical fabric itself.

---

1   The editor wishes to thank the relevant authors for permission to reprint their articles in English translation for an international readership.

The two great national Nielsen projects—the Letters Edition and the Collected Works – are both proceeding well.

The Letters Edition was consolidated in autumn 2007 through a bequest from the Carl Nielsen-Legat that has secured funding for the first five volumes, of which volume 3, covering the period 1906-1910, was published in summer 2007. The first three volumes are reviewed by David Fanning in this issue of *Carl Nielsen Studies* (see pp. 111-115).

The Carl Nielsen Edition approaches its conclusion: three large volumes were published in late autumn 2007 containing incidental music; hereafter only two volumes of cantatas and one volume with *Juvenilia et addenda* remain, in addition to Nielsen's more than 300 songs. These works will be published during the course of 2008 and early 2009, after which Nielsen's complete works will be available in a scholarly critical edition in 30 volumes, published over the period 1997-2009.

Both projects will provide scholars and musicians with insight into Nielsen's life and work to a degree which will hopefully inspire further research in Nielsen-related areas.

The next issue of the current journal, *Carl Nielsen Studies 4*, is expected to be published in 2009, and will focus upon the preceding 15 years' work with *The Carl Nielsen Edition* in recognition of the project's completion. *Studies 4* will also be open to articles of a more general nature without particular reference to the collected edition. Material for submission should be sent to *Carl Nielsen Studies*, The Royal Library, PB 2149, DK 1017 or via email to nk@kb.dk.

CARL NIELSEN UNDER THE INFLUENCE
Some New Sources for the First Symphony[1]

By David Fanning

What really matters is never passed on from one composer to another.[2]

Alfred Schnittke's warning is provocative. He was talking about a specific musical idea that Shostakovich heard in one of his student works and then recycled in his own Eleventh Symphony. Schnittke wanted to make the point that such borrowing – whether deliberate or inadvertent – was not shameful, and that the meaning of the borrower's work was not dependent on it. What 'matters' – to take Schnittke's observation a stage further – is what the borrower does with an idea rather than where he takes it from.

And yet Schnittke himself was one of the most voracious and explicit borrowers in the history of music. It would be hard to know where to begin with many of his works without pondering the significance of their quotations and stylistic allusions.

So with a wary but open mind, and without prejudice as to how much or how little the process may ultimately tell us, I propose to investigate some musical sources for Nielsen's music, especially for the First Symphony. My only criteria are that his borrowings (if such they be) should not have been investigated before, and that their identification should illuminate some aspect of the beneficiary work beyond the mere fact of the borrowing.

The 'sources' referred to in the title are hypothetical, because I cannot prove that Nielsen even knew most of the pieces I'm going to mention. And I add the phrase 'under the influence' for two reasons: because he himself occasionally used metaphors of intoxication when describing his music, and because I suspect that musical influence was not something he always absorbed soberly and calculatedly, but that he may just as often have found it de-inhibiting and liberating.

---

1 This article is a lightly revised version of an essay with the same title in Anne Ørbæk Jensen et al. (eds.), *Musikvidenskabelige kompositioner: Festskrift til Niels Krabbe* (Musicological Compositions. Festskrift for Niels Krabbe), Copenhagen 2006, 437-455.
2 'Alfred Schnittke, in conversation with Alexander Ivashkin'. See Ivashkin (ed.), *A Schnittke Reader*, Bloomington 2002, 17.

The main part of this essay, then, will be about Nielsen and the Ecstasy, as opposed to the Anxiety of Influence. Harold Bloom's classic text of literary criticism has filtered into musicology via a number of widely read studies.[3] But his terminology is disconcertingly negative. Take 'misreading', for example, which Bloom uses to cover instances of creative reappropriation of artistic statements. The word implies incompetence, which seems unhelpful, to say the least, when applied to artists of the stature of Schubert, Bruckner, Brahms and Mahler (to mention some of the most obvious 'misreaders' of Beethoven). Whereas I would prefer to celebrate the similarities. If those similarities are conscious, then they may be springboards to flights of imagination that, after all, have to take off from somewhere.[4] And even if they are 'merely' unconscious, or even entirely coincidental, then there is still something here that is worthy of our attention, namely the existence of archetypal sources of musical expression. In fact whatever the status of the similarities, their identification has a role to play in our understanding of where pieces of music come from and what makes them unique; since to grasp the origins of an idea, or even its affinities, is to take a step towards seeing more clearly what the composer does with it and how he makes it his own, hence what his unique voice is and what he says with it. And that is what I believe (and I believe Schnittke believed) 'matters'.

How may we recognise influence as such? How might we distinguish between its manifestations as quotation, allusion and unconscious affinity? How to distinguish all of those from mere coincidence? And even when a specific identification seems unequivocally positive, what is the point of it? It is hard to know how to deal with such questions in a scholarly way. Although there is a sizable literature on the topic of musical quotation,[5] there is nothing that really tells us how to handle the issue sensitively or how to avoid the obvious pitfalls.

There was a time when Nielsen commentators routinely noted allusions or similarities to earlier music, in the apparent belief that to do so was self-evidently a good thing, necessitating no further comment. Ludvig Dolleris's commentaries are especially rich in this respect, and Frede Schandorf Petersen's contributions to the life-and-works study with Torben Meyer are not far behind.[6] Robert Simpson sprinkled his discussions with such observations, though more often than not referring to

3 Such as Mark Evans Bonds, *After Beethoven: Imperatives of Originality in the Symphony*, Cambridge, Mass. 1996, and Joseph Straus, *Remaking the Past, Musical Modernism and the Influence of the Tonal Tradition*, Cambridge, Mass. 1990

4 This is the argument advanced in Charles Rosen, 'Influence: Plagiarism and Inspiration', *19th-Century Music*, IV/2 (1980), 87-100.

5 See Bibliography in J. Peter Burkholder, 'Quotation', in Stanley Sadie and John Tyrrell (eds.), *The New Grove Dictionary of Music and Musicians*, 2nd edn., London 2001, vol. 20, 689-691.

6 Ludvig Dolleris, *Carl Nielsen: en Musikografi*, Odense 1949; Torben Meyer & Frede Schandorf Petersen, *Carl Nielsen. Kunstneren og Mennesket*, Copenhagen 1947-1948.

general affinities rather than to specific pieces.[7] Occasionally contributors to *Carl Nielsen Studies* have themselves added to the store.[8]

But as has been pointed out, while this mode of commentary has thrived in history-of-art scholarship, it has significantly declined in musicology and literary studies,[9] partly, perhaps, because of a general narrowing of horizons under the pressure to specialize, but partly also on good intellectual grounds. For this is an area fraught with traps for the unwary, perhaps the most conspicuous being that of wishful thinking. When Jørgen I. Jensen, in his fascinating and path-breaking study, appends a long list of themes that descend from the fifth degree of the scale to the tonic, the idea is to point to something that is personal to Nielsen.[10] In fact that self-same shape has long been recognised as personal to Schumann too – possibly as a means of coded communication with Clara Wieck.[11] And a few moments' thought would confirm that this shape is an archetype of tonal music, not much more characteristic of Nielsen than of anyone else. If we want to look for more significant affinities, then it would probably be better to do so at the level of musical gesture and texture. And even here, Brahms's withering put-down, '*Das sieht jeder Esel*' – referring to the similarity between the main finale themes of his First Symphony and Beethoven's Ninth – lies in wait for all identifications that are just too obvious. Moreover, some similarities that may *seem* obvious must almost certainly be coincidences, as the late Jonathan Kramer noted in pointing out a resemblance between the 'Humoreske' from Nielsen's Sixth Symphony and the theme for the duck in Prokofiev's *Peter and the Wolf*, composed ten years later.[12] In other instances the resemblance may be so tenuous that only the identifier himself believes in its significance, while readers may attribute it to an over-active imagination. Composers themselves do not necessarily hear what is obvious to their commentators. Admittedly sometimes one suspects that composers' scepticism may betoken a certain overprotectiveness towards their 'originality' or 'inspiration', which may go as much for the constructional processes of their music as for the ideas themselves. Stravinsky was perhaps the most notorious denier of the patent and provable origin of his themes, and he has been posthumously exposed;[13] that exposing is one type of contribution musicolo-

---

7   Robert Simpson, *Carl Nielsen: Symphonist*, 2nd edn., London 1979.

8   Notably Friedhelm Krummacher, 'Steps to Modernism: Carl Nielsen's String Quartets', *Carl Nielsen Studies*, 2 (2005), 89-131.

9   Rosen, *op. cit.*, 88.

10 Jørgen I. Jensen, *Carl Nielsen – Danskeren* [Nielsen – the Dane], Copenhagen 1991, 467-475.

11 See Eric Sams, 'Did Schumann use Ciphers?', *The Musical Times* 106 (1965) 584–591; R. Larry Todd, 'On Quotation in Schumann's Music', in *idem*, *Schumann and his World*, Princeton 1994, 80–112.

12 Mina Miller (ed.), *The Nielsen Companion*, London 1994, 327.

13 To take just one famous case, see Lawrence Morton, 'Footnotes to Stravinsky Studies: *Le sacre du printemps*', *Tempo* no.128 (1979) 9–16; Richard Taruskin, 'Russian Folk Melodies in *The Rite of Spring*', *Journal of the American Musicological Society* 33 (1980), 501–543.

gists can make towards uncovering the truth – or unmasking the untruth — of music's origins. But it is not my purpose in this article. I would rather take composerly scepticism as a warning against musicological self-aggrandisement.

According to Charles Rosen,

> In discussing musical influence in music, it would be wise to refuse in advance to consider the work of adolescent composers... [since w]ith the startling exception of Mendelssohn, a very young composer has no style of his own, and he is forced to get one somewhere else. His models have largely a biographical, but not much critical, significance – he may, indeed, reject his early models by the time he reaches his majority.'[14]

All true. But in his First Symphony, composed mainly between the ages of 26 and 28, Nielsen had most certainly reached his majority. A year after its completion, he himself wrote to his benefactor William Behrend acknowledging the influences of Beethoven, Brahms, Grieg and Johan Svendsen on his early works, and declaring various degrees of respect for César Franck, Wagner and Bruckner.[15] And many commentators have detected the presence of some of these and other related models behind the First Symphony, if only in very general terms. Typical of such remarks are those of Simpson: '[Nielsen's] debt to Brahms is often obvious, though his scoring, with its open bluntness of sound, is more like Dvořák's', while the first movement exposition material 'may remind one at times of Brahms or Dvořák (with a possible Russian influence – perhaps Borodin – in [the second subject]).'[16] Dolleris picked up an echo of Svendsen (conductor of the premiere of Nielsen's Symphony) in the third movement, but again without mentioning any specific piece.[17] Interspersed between Frede Schandorf Petersen's more detailed comments on the First Symphony, Torben Meyer also mentions Svendsen, as a model for form rather than style, but he adds that at this stage, 'Brahms is probably the only composer whose stylistic line leads to and is continued by Carl Nielsen.'[18] I myself have offered the reminder that in November 1890, by which time sporadic ideas for the Symphony were already taking shape, Nielsen had set himself the task of copying out from memory the first movement of Beethoven's Fifth Symphony.[19] Not that there are obvious traces of Beethoven's

---

14 Rosen, *op. cit.*, 88.
15 See John Fellow (ed.), *Carl Nielsen Brevudgaven*, vol. 1 1886-1897, Copenhagen 2005, 407-408.
16 Simpson, *op. cit.*, 23, 26.
17 Dolleris, *op. cit.*, 32.
18 Meyer & Schandorf Petersen, *op. cit.*, 110.
19 Torben Schousboe (ed.), *Carl Nielsen: Dagbøger og brevveksling med Anne Marie Carl-Nielsen*, Copenhagen 1983, 24; John Fellow (2005) *op. cit.*, 142.

themes; but that work is the *locus classicus* of thematic economy, and its dynamism and thrust find some echo in Nielsen's own first movement.

But there comes a point when all this generalized talk of affinities ceases to have much value. If we want to go deeper in our understanding, we have to take a deep breath and dive into musical analysis. Or else – and this is what I shall now attempt – we have to ask what specific pieces Nielsen might have had on his mind. I have ventured one instance from Svendsen (whose Second Symphony very definitely influenced Nielsen's *Symphonic Rhapsody*, to the extent that Nielsen was moved to abandon his piece for that very reason). But, with apologies, I am going to withdraw that identification below, in favour of something rather more direct in its resemblance and more suggestive in its implications.

Brigands and Dynamite

Before that, a thought on Nielsen's superb opening theme. It is not Beethoven, not Brahms, not Dvořák, and not Svendsen who stand behind it. At least it is not any of those so much as Berlioz and the main theme of his 'Orgy of the Brigands' finale in *Harold in Italy* (*Ex. 1*). The resemblances, especially in terms of rhythmic gesture, are surely compelling enough to the eye not to require spelling out; though I cannot resist adding that the metronome mark – ♩ = 104 – as well as the tonality and metre, is identical. Even the famous disjunction between the opening chord and the main tonality is there. The tied and syncopated figures in Berlioz's theme are precisely what Nielsen uses to drive the central section of his movement towards its climax (see bb. 153-164); and in a tranquillised form they become the initiating motif for the second movement (see *Ex.1c*).

Ex. 1a: *Berlioz,* Harold in Italy, *finale opening*

Ex. 1b: *Nielsen, Symphony No. 1, first movement, opening*

Ex. 1c: *Nielsen, Symphony No. 1, second movement, opening*

Given that there is no evidence that Nielsen actually knew *Harold in Italy*, there is nothing more to be said about the status of this similarity as conscious allusion or co-incidence. Even if it was conscious, that would not necessarily mean that any of the brigandly or orgiastic associations of Berlioz's finale necessarily carry over into Nielsen's theme, or that they need to in anyone else's reading of it; still less that there are any half-hidden Byronic topics needing to be teased out of Nielsen's symphony as a whole.

But that is not to say that there is no deeper point to the similarity. First, it prompts some thoughts about Nielsen's curious *Allegro orgoglioso* marking, without which few listeners would surely choose 'proud' as a description of the music's character. The music radiates energy, to be sure, but not pride, at least not in the sense of self-satisfaction. So in the light of Berlioz's *frenetico*, I wonder if Nielsen's *orgoglioso* may be there partly as a means of moderating any instinct a conductor might have for making the character too excitable — too Berliozian. If the *allegro* had been left unqualified (or with the composer's original *marcato*[20]), a touch of *frenetico* in performance would have been a perfectly understandable response. In line with this speculation, I recall that Nielsen himself on at least one occasion after the premiere dropped *orgoglioso* in favour of *moderato*, at the same time adding the proviso to his third movement, *non è scherzo*.[21]

---

20 *Carl Nielsen Works*, II/1, (2001), 162. For changes to the remaining movement superscriptions, see *ibid.*, xii.
21 Peter Hauge, Preface to *Carl Nielsen Works*, II/1, (2001), xix.

The Berlioz example offers other tempting paths towards the inner workings of Nielsen's *Allegro*. Looking away from the page and reconstructing the Brigands' theme from memory, I suspect many of us would mis-remember the opening chord as a tonic G minor. Even if we remembered it correctly as a dominant, we might naturally assume that it comes on the up-beat — where the textbooks say a dominant in a perfect cadence should be, and where it is 'correctly' located later on when the movement gets properly launched. Berlioz's initial placing of his emphatic dominant seventh on the *down*-beat is in itself enough to set his Brigands' theme on an excitingly unstable platform, and his immediate plunge into an unharmonised tonic-triad-based theme confirms that something wild and wilful is in the air. All this is taken up and tweaked by Nielsen with his C-major *premier coup d'archet*. With that bold 'tonic-equals-subdominant' affirmation he immediately takes us into a world in motion. Like Berlioz, he as it were puts an exclamation mark before his first word. As the symphony progresses, Nielsen's invocation of Berliozian thematic energy will in due course unite at the highest conceptual level with the large-scale architectural energy of the off-tonic opening gambit (as in Beethoven's Op. 5 Cello Sonata, Fourth Piano Concerto, Second 'Razumovsky' Quartet and 'Archduke' Trio). As with Beethoven, so with Nielsen, an exclamation mark thus broadens out, metaphorically, to motivate an entire musical drama.

Berlioz's theme is brilliantly suited to launching his finale, just as all the above-cited Beethoven off-tonic openings are. But what boldness for Nielsen to use the same intonations to launch a *first* movement. Of course, this was 1892, or thereabouts, not 1834 (Berlioz *Harold*) or 1796 (Beethoven Op. 5). The world had moved on, and musical language with it. Merely to imitate without intensification, however perceptively, would have been to settle for complacency. Whereas it is Nielsen's willingness to take risks that marks him out – along with Dvořák, Tchaikovsky, Bruckner, Mahler, Sibelius and not so many others — from the hundreds of fellow-symphonists active in the 1890s. In this respect, the most enthusiastic review of the 14 March 1894 premiere hit the nail on the head: 'Restless and reckless in its harmonies and modulations, yet overall as wonderfully innocent and unselfconscious as a child playing with dynamite.'[22] Except that the game may not have been as innocent and unconscious as all that.

Did Nielsen bring it off? Perhaps he was not best advised to follow Berlioz in letting his theme sit down so firmly in the tonic at the end of 20 bars. Berlioz's theme does so only because his broader strategy is to pass in review the main themes from his previous movements before launching the finale properly, at which point the full

---

22 *Uroligt og hensynsløst i Harmoni og Modulation, men altsammen dog saa forunderlig uskyldigt og ubevidst, som saa man et Barn lege med Dynamit.* Charles Kjerulf in *Politiken*, 15.3.1894, cited in *Carl Nielsen Works*, II/1, xiii (translation adapted).

close is swept away in a torrent of modulatory energy. So I draw the opposite conclusion from Simpson, who felt that 'The breadth [!] of [Nielsen's] conception is immediately shown by the fact that this [idea] is the start of a 20-bar sentence for the full orchestra ... ending with a firm G minor cadence.'[23] Since when did a 20-bar opening sentence indicate breadth of conception? At any rate it hardly did so in 1894. If anything, it is surely Nielsen's terseness and concentration that deserve praise. Making his symphonic debut, Nielsen still had a somewhat compartmentalized approach to large-scale form, though what he did in compensation is remarkable enough, as I have probed on more than one occasion.[24] That is really no surprise at a historical juncture where half a century of the Leipzig-centred domesticated version of the symphony had all but extinguished the flaming immediacy of its Beethoven/Berlioz incarnations (recall the memorable encapsulation in a contemporary description of Nielsen's Danish symphonic godfather Niels Gade – the one potential influence that Nielsen most emphatically wanted not to be constrained by – as 'Mendelssohnacidic Schumannoxide').[25] All I am really claiming is that ideas such as Berlioz's Brigands' theme may have given Nielsen a decisive impulse and spur to his imagination and craftsmanship, inspiring him with the recognition that there was a kind of excitement and intensity waiting to be explored in music, in a quite different dimension from the prevailing Wagner/Brahms polarity.

Nielsen did include Berlioz in his famous list of those artists who had 'brandished the hardest fist [and]... given their times a black eye' and who would therefore be remembered longest.[26] But he rarely noted his specific contacts with Berlioz's music, hardly ever praised it and only ever conducted the odd overture or excerpt from larger works. Yet the affinities are compelling and multi-faceted. Berlioz and Nielsen are two of the great adventurer-composers in the history of music. Both were impelled by the example of Beethoven towards a rhythmic style that is invigorating to the point of wildness; both took an empirical, emancipated view of harmony and tonality; both wrote an abundance of warm, tender, even amorous music, yet with a kind of chasteness that spurns languishing and erotic explicitness; both had an unsentimental yet passionate identification with the pastoral, and so on. Nielsen certainly knew the *Symphonie fantastique* as early as February 1891, when he heard it in Leipzig, just before he began work on his First Symphony.[27] And leaving the First Symphony to one side, it

23 Simpson, *op. cit.*, 25.
24 David Fanning, 'Carl Nielsen's Progressive Thematicism', in Mina Miller, *op. cit.*, 173-178; 'Carl Nielsen and Early Twentieth-Century Musical/Aesthetic Theory', *Carl Nielsen Studies*, 1 (2003), 12-13.
25 Cited in Paul Henry Lang, *Music in Western Civilization*, London 1963 (originally published 1941), 959.
26 Schousboe, *op. cit.*, 29; Fellow (2005), *op. cit.*, 160.
27 Schousboe, *op. cit.*, 43; Fellow (2005), *op. cit.*, 196.

seems a reasonable hypothesis that the writing for timpani in the *Fantastique* left a deep imprint on Nielsen's subconscious, as did its intervallic distortions, its antiphonal effects and its crazy fugue, all found in the 'Witches' Sabbath' finale. Of course in saying this, the Nielsen example I have in mind is the finale of *The Inextinguishable*. Also, Nielsen conducted excerpts from Berlioz's *Romeo and Juliet* Symphony on more than one occasion, and he could hardly have failed to observe in that score the repeated-note chimes on antique cymbals and the bottom B-flats for bassoon (representing the soldier's snores) in the 'Queen Mab' Scherzo, the very sounds that would provide the frame for his *Sinfonia semplice*. He could equally have derived some of the bizarrerie of the 'Humoreske' in that work from the convulsive music for Juliet's awakening in the last instrumental movement of *Romeo and Juliet*. Historically the Berlioz influence may be at its most conspicuous in such melodrama specialists as Liszt, Tchaikovsky and Mahler. But surely the Frenchman would have recognised a kindred spirit in the Nielsen of the 'Choleric' Temperament, the Clarinet Concerto, the *Presto* fugue in the Fifth Symphony, numerous other structure-intensifying fugatos, and so on.

Symphonies and Mountains

Svendsen himself must have been a Berlioz enthusiast, if pieces like his *Carnival in Paris* are anything to go by. This 'Episode', composed in 1872, is very conspicuously a Scandinavian answer to Berlioz's *Roman Carnival* Overture, and Nielsen was captivated by it in 1890,[28] just as Wagner had been in the 1870s. I have previously cited *Carnival in Paris* as a likely source for one of the most characteristic harmonic progressions in Nielsen's First Symphony.[29]

The progression in question features in all four of Nielsen's movements, almost always at the same pitch level of E-flat last-inversion dominant-seventh moving to C major (as in the first movement: bb. 61-63, 194-196, 334-335, 338-339; second movement: bb. 31, 70; third movement: bb. 11-14; 92-97, 183-185, 203-206; finale: bb. 254-270). From the First Symphony this progression passes down as a Nielsen fingerprint to the first movements of *The Four Temperaments* (De fire Temperamenter) and the *Sinfonia Espansiva*. The instance shown in *Ex. 2a* from the third movement of the First Symphony may be tiny, but to anyone familiar with his work the sound of it instantly says 'early Nielsen' (another instance is shown in *Ex. 5b* below). The way Nielsen frames this progression and uses it as a pivotal force in the broader scheme of things makes it a compelling part of the First Symphony's overall tonal journey, bringing as it does constant reminders of the initially anomalous C-major that is eventually to serve as the destination of the finale.

---

28 Schousboe, *op. cit.*, 33; Fellow (2005), *op. cit.*, 179.

29 Fanning, 'Carl Nielsen', in Robert Layton (ed.), *A Companion to the Symphony*, London 1993, 354.

In fact Svendsen's *Carnival* has a far weaker claim to parenthood than Liszt's tone-poem *Ce qu'on entend sur la montagne*, otherwise known as the *Bergsymphonie* (Mountain Symphony). The progression materialises from the mysterious shimmering of the opening bars, which are presumably a response to the opening of Victor Hugo's poem printed in the score: '*O altitudo! | Avez-vous quelquefois, calme et silencieux, | Monté sur la montagne, en présence des cieux?*' A choir of woodwind and low horns announces the progression, in the carefully framed manner of Nielsen's third movement (*Ex. 2b*). A few pages further on in Liszt's score, at the *poco a poco più moto*, the same progression may be found stretched out and coloured by trombones and tuba, to complete the resemblance with Nielsen's third movement.

Ex. 2a: *Nielsen, Symphony No. 1, third movement, bb. 92-94*

Ex. 2b: *Liszt,* Mountain Symphony, *bb. 9-12*

Liszt was another of Nielsen's non-favourite composers, not even featuring alongside Berlioz in the famous list of 'fist-brandishers'. There is no record of Nielsen's ever having conducted a note of Liszt's music, and the *Mountain Symphony* does not figure in his copious diary entries. Moreover, in an entry of 7 November 1890, he referred to the tone-poem *Tasso* 'a piece of sh** ...; he can't pull the wool over my... ears',[30] though

---

30 Schousboe, *op. cit.*, 25; Fellow (2005), *op. cit.*, 143: *Det er noget Sk...; han kan ikke stikke mig Blaar i ... Ørerne.*

a few weeks later he did note the Third Hungarian Rhapsody as 'good'. Nielsen even took Liszt as a counter-example to musical good taste, when he referred disparagingly to music that was rather too inclined to pictorialism, 'but that at least never screams and screeches as in Liszt's poster-art, which seems to be all the rage these days'.[31]

This may be the point at which to side-step once again away from Nielsen's First Symphony and to mention the arch-pictorialist Richard Strauss – also a target for Nielsen's scorn (but occasional enthusiasm, as for *Tod und Verklärung* in 1891),[32] and whose personal encounter with Nielsen in 1894 left an extremely negative impression.[33] The Bavarian may also have to be credited with one of Nielsen's most famous ideas. Coincidentally, it concerns another sunrise in the mountains, in yet another programmatic symphony. In Strauss's *Alpine Symphony* (rehearsal no. 7 in the score), the full-orchestral A-major scalic descent and dotted rhythms prefigure the redemptive theme of *The Inextinguishable* (Det Uudslukkelige, – see especially fig. 11 in Nielsen's score, where it appears in A major) (*Ex. 3*). This resemblance was picked up as early as 1949, when Dolleris sought (not very convincingly) to defend Nielsen from possible charges of plagiarism by reminding his readers of a previous scalic descent in the coda to the 'Phlegmatic Temperament'.[34] In fact few listeners who know both the Nielsen and the Strauss can have failed to spot the resemblance. However, proving or disproving plagiarism would be a Sherlock Holmesian task. Strauss's symphony was completed in February 1915, premiered on 28 October and published the same year. Nielsen's concept for *The Inextinguishable* goes back at least as far as May 1914, but he seems to have been uncertain about its progress as late as March 1915, and there

Festes Zeitmass, mässig langsam

Ex. 3a: *Strauss, Alpine Symphony, 'Sonnenaufgang'*

31 *som dog aldrig skriger og hviner som i den Liszt'ske Plakat-Kunst, der ellers for Øjeblikket er i Mode allevegne.* 'Svensk Musikfest', *Politiken*, 14.6.1906, reprinted in Fellow (ed.), *Carl Nielsen til sin samtid*, Copenhagen 1999, 89.
32 Schousboe, *op. cit.*, 45, 46; Fellow (2005), *op. cit.*, 207.
33 Schousboe, *op. cit.*, 111-112; Fellow (2005), *op. cit.*, 372.
34 Dolleris, *op. cit.*, 205.

is no evidence of notated material before that date. He could therefore conceivably have pinched his theme from Strauss (clearly it could not have been *vice versa*). But whether that is a more likely scenario than both composers drawing on an available archetype or on some yet-to-be-identified specific source, remains an open question. For example, compare the theme for horns and tubas three minutes or so into the Adagio of Bruckner's Ninth Symphony, described by the composer himself as a 'Farewell to Life' (*Ex. 3c*).[35]

Ex. 3b: *Nielsen* The Inextinguishable, *first movement*

Ex. 3c: *Bruckner, Symphony No. 9, third movement*

---

35 See Robert Simpson, *The Essence of Bruckner*, London 1992, 221.

Symphonies *à la russe*

Sibelius and Nielsen were not the only symphonists born in 1865. In St. Petersburg, Alexander Glazunov was destined to become one of the defining musical voices of Russia's Silver Age. 45 years later his symphonic output came to an abrupt halt. But at the time of Nielsen's First Symphony, with four symphonies under his belt, Glazunov already had a strong claim to the mantle of Tchaikovsky. He was off the symphonic starting-blocks as early as 1882, at the age of 17, more than ten years before Nielsen. That work still radiates warmth, freshness and energy, especially in its first movement, notated in a swinging 6/8 metre with plentiful hemiolas, that is something of a missing link between Schumann's 'Rhenish' and the athletic triple-time motion of Nielsen's *Espansiva* first movement, the finales of his Fourth and Fifth Symphonies, and above all the third movement of No. 1.

I would happily pass over the general similarities of character and motion in these movements as no more than generic, were it not for the beginning of Glazunov's development section, where the melody passes down from octave to leading-note and flattened leading-note on the way to a sequential restatement. Nielsen's sequence rises rather than falls, but otherwise the resemblance is striking; I have taken the liberty of renotating Glazunov's 6/8 as 6/4 (*Ex. 4*).

Ex. 4a: *Glazunov, Symphony No. 1, first movement, metrically renotated*

Ex. 4b: *Nielsen, Symphony No. 1, third movement (opening of development section in both cases)*

The flattened seventh is a frequently cited marker of Nielsen's musical language; it was somewhat hyperbolically discussed by Dolleris as '*det antikke Toneprincip*' (the antique melodic principle). But in fact it is not so remarkable, and the Glazunov instance could easily be multiplied from within the 19th-century symphonic repertoire. It is the combination with the chromatic descent and the broader sequential progression that makes the resemblance in *Ex. 4* so persuasive, and that emboldens me to pick out in addition the climax of Glazunov's development section and compare it to the highpoints of Nielsen's exposition and reprise (*Ex. 5*). Admittedly the first movement of Beethoven's Seventh Symphony supplies a model for the driving rhythm in both cases. And the real point is that for all the surface similarity with Glazunov, Nielsen's embodiment of the 'apotheosis of the Dance' (Wagner's description of the Beethoven, of course) is far more crisp. Anyone who doubts Nielsen's brusque concentration or the power of its structural embodiment, by comparison with Glazunov's easy conventionality, need only expand the focus from *Ex. 5* and consider how those passages are prepared and extended.

Ex. 5a: *Glazunov, Symphony No. 1, first movement, development climax, metrically renotated*

Ex. 5b: *Nielsen, Symphony No. 1, third movement, exposition climax*

Symphonies on home ground

Glazunov and Nielsen is not a conjunction to be found in the musicological literature, apart from their joint participation in the 1928 Schubert competition and
their contributions to a German newspaper's compilation of comments on the
Beethoven centenary the previous year.[36] Whereas there is a clear thread connect-
ing the careers of Nielsen and Peter Erasmus Lange-Müller. The two were often to be
found on the same concert programmes, and despite fundamental differences of
temperament they were more often than not respectful of one another's work.
There would be nothing more natural than to find pre-echoes of Nielsen in the two
symphonies Lange-Müller composed in the 1880s, but it was not until their appearance on CD – the symphonies remain unpublished in score form – that most of us
had the chance to judge. The First was premiered in the Musikforening on 11 February 1882 and was also heard at Tivoli later that year. Whether or not Nielsen heard
it by the time of the First Symphony, he could conceivably have known the piano
duet score (published in February 1882 according to Dan Fog's unpublished Lange-
Müller work catalogue) and he would have at least eight opportunities to hear the
work in the early years of the new century. Conductor Douglas Bostock has picked
up on the abrupt opposition between solo clarinet and full orchestra just before the
middle section of Lange-Müller's slow movement as a likely inspiration for passages
in the first movement development section in *The Inextinguishable*; and he suggests a
connection between the main finale theme and the opening of Nielsen's First Symphony (*Ex. 6*, cf. *Ex. 1b*).

Ex. 6: *Lange-Müller, Symphony No. 1, fourth movement, bb. 13-16*

It is true that the motif bracketed on *Ex. 6* (compare Nielsen's second and third bars)
becomes the main driving force for Lange-Müller's finale. But both he and Nielsen
could easily have got it from other sources, such as the finale of Schumann's D minor

36 Fellow (1999), *op. cit.*, 431.

Symphony. Even so, the point could be proposed that, as with the Berlioz Brigands' theme, Nielsen here took an idea usually associated with a sense of cutting-loose – typical of finales – and unlocked its potential for the more abstract energy of a symphonic first movement.

Yet I find that my ear is caught rather more by the passage from just before the middle section of Lange-Müller's slow third movement, which irresistibly recalls one of Nielsen's most characterstic turns of phrase, the plagal cadence with the flattened seventh (also to be found in Dvořák, of course – his Cello Concerto is virtually an encyclopedia of the plagal cadence). Nielsen repeatedly uses the subdominant with flattened seventh to lend a mixture of wonder and nobility to his phrases, most strikingly in the slow movement of the First Symphony at the retransition – it is partly his uncharacteristic *nobile* marking for the actual return of the theme that prompts me to use that description. And his most shattering use of this harmony is at the *glorioso* climax in the finale of *The Inextinguishable*, where all four horns blaze out the subdominant seventh – in the same key as Lange-Müller, as it happens, but also (as distinct from Lange-Müller) with a mass of larger-scale structural forces coalescing at this point, as well as the horns' carried-over E, making this one of the most spine-tingling moments in all of Nielsen's music (*Ex. 7*).

Lange-Müller's Second Symphony, also in D minor, was heard in Copenhagen at a Philharmonic Concert on 27 April 1889 that Nielsen could easily have attended. Here the first movement – in 6/4 with plentiful hemiolas – brings numerous anticipations of Nielsen's third movement, even before the specific passage Bostock notes, where the tempo slows for a moment of chorale-like reflection before the recapitulation. Similarly one could look at Lange-Müller's 3/2 finale and draw numerous connections with the first movement of *The Inextinguishable*.

Ex. 7a: *Lange-Müller, Symphony No. 1, third movement, bb. 80-89*

Ex. 7b: *Nielsen, Symphony No. 1, second movement, bb. 53-57*

Ex. 7c: *Nielsen, Symphony No. 4, fourth movement, bb. 827-838*

It is hard not to ponder that if this single compact disc of previously forgotten and unpublished music has so much to suggest to us about the origins of Nielsen's early style, what further riches might there be among the work of the numerous other composers active at the time, for instance among those discussed in the 550 pages of Gerhardt Lynge's *Danske Komponister i det 20. Aarhundredes Begyndelse* (Danish Composers at the Beginning of the 20th. Century, Aarhus, 1917). And there is really no need to fear the results of such enquiry. If a little bit of de-mythologising is called for – if we no longer credit Nielsen with the invention *ex nihilo* of ideas that we would like to think of as quintessentially Nielsenesque – then that is merely part and parcel of a process of growing up. In any case, as I have tried to show, the identification of similarity and/or influence is only the means towards more ambitious ends, as expressed by Charles Rosen in conclusion to his 1980 benchmark article on the topic of influence:

> What Brahms had to say about his relation to history and to the past, he let his music say for him. This goes to show that when the study of sources is at its most interesting, it becomes indistinguishable from pure musical analysis.[37]

Nearly 30 years on, it may be harder to think of 'pure musical analysis' as an unblemished positive. But Rosen's meaning is clear. All paths that connect where music comes from to a rich experience of it have to be good. It that sense, what passes from one composer to another really does matter.

A B S T R A C T

Nielsen's general musical affinities are often mentioned, and in some cases they are well documented. But even in a work as characterful and characteristic as the First Symphony, there are several *prima facie* cases of allusion to specific works – from Berlioz to Lange-Müller – that have not previously been identified. The point of proposing and discussing them here is not to downgrade the originality of Nielsen's symphonic breakthrough piece, but rather to lead towards a closer understanding of what makes it unique, by showing how it borrows ideas only to go beyond them and to reveal new potential.

---

37 Rosen, *op. cit.*, 100.

A PATRIOTIC SONG
AND ITS CONSEQUENCES:
'Du danske Mand' through hundred years[1]

By John Fellow

Danish identity has come out for another round and once again has us pinned to the canvas. We now have ourselves a national cultural canon,[2] which includes the high chair,[3] the lego brick, Nielsen's *John the Roadman* (Jens Vejmand) and *The Inextinguishable*: Danishness from the cradle to the grave, and beyond the death of the individual.

Articles, dissertations and books are being written about Danishness in music and literature – and in Sandholmlejren.[4] Danish identity is discussed and problematised; some speak for it, some against, some believe in it, others deny its existence; some think that people who view it ironically are nonetheless expressing themselves in terms of Danishness. Whether you are an old Dane nor a new Dane, there is no way of avoiding Danishness. In Denmark eternal Danishness is a fact of life you have to come to terms with. "Follow the law of the land or get out", as the old Danes used to say. In Denmark the law is Danishness: for or against – the choice is yours.

Those of us old enough to have frequented the public Danish school system in the 1950s and 60s already then learned a kind of *modus vivendi* with Danishness. We had grown out of high chairs and lego, and those few of us who discovered *The Inextinguishable* made that discovery outside school and as a contrast to all the pop music that most of us, also away from school, surrendered to. There was no music education at state

1 This article is based in part on a talk given in the Concert Hall of Danish Radio on 3 October 2001 to mark the 70th anniversary of Nielsen's death.

2 In December 2004, the Danish Minister for Culture, Brian Mikkelsen, announced plans to compile a cultural canon for Denmark. Seven committees, each consisting of five members, were formed, with a remit to choose 12 works that would define what is characteristic and distinctive about each of the arts in Denmark (the music committee in the end chose 12 popular and 12 classical works). 175,000 copies of the resulting book were published in August 2006 and made available free to schools and colleges.

3 Nanna Ditzel's design of 1955 was famous in Denmark for introducing high-quality design into furniture for children.

4 Formerly a barracks in the north of Zealand, now accommodation for asylum seekers.

primary and lower-secondary schools in those days. While Shakespeare, Goethe and Dostoevsky were at least named, Bach, Beethoven and Brahms did not exist. At school we had singing lessons, in which we learned and sang hymns, psalms and Danish folk-songs *ad infinitum*, in every single singing class and sometimes also in some of the other lessons. How many times we sang Nielsen and Drachmann's *Thou Danish Man* (Du danske Mand), no one can say; it was certainly many times, and it was not an expression of any form of conscious acknowledgment of any form of Danishness.

We knew the words by heart. Psalm verses and rote learning had been part of our education from the first day at school. There was not so much beating about the bush then; learning and understanding did not always have much to do with one another. We learned psalm verses the way the Chinese digitise Danish dictionaries: error-free transcription, precisely because we understood nothing. On the other hand, many years later walking down the street we might suddenly be reminded of the old words and with wonder understand the deeper meaning in the impossible sentence, 'The Lord himself on Zion's mountains is shield and sword for his people.'[5] What a load of drivel we learned back then – so most of us probably thought – while one of us perhaps got annoyed over the fact it had taken so long to reach the foothills of Zion, now that he finally understood. Maybe one day in the middle of a street in China the light will dawn on a Chinaman, and he will realise that he has a problem with Danishness.

We didn't have any problem with understanding the text of *Du danske Mand*, and when we got to it yet again just before the bell rang to signal the end of the lesson, we suddenly woke up and bawled along with cheerful irony 'about our old mother'.[6] Perhaps we had to sing *Thou Danish Man* so often because the old teacher had realised that with this song he could even get the apathetic boys to join in the choir. No one took *Thou Danish Man* entirely seriously. If anyone had asked us whether we were sitting there with our bawling and asserting our connection with Danishness, or on the other hand whether we perhaps believed that we were undermining Danish identity with our irony, we would undoubtedly have answered, once we had stopped to think about it: 'the latter!'; and immediately we would have felt a touch of bad conscience about poking fun at the nation's past.

Times were changing; nationalism was passé, the future was becoming international, not yet global, and this development fortunately allowed us easily to forget everything about bad conscience and sacrilege with regard to *Thou Danish Man* .

Then in the early 1970s came the campaign for and against Denmark's membership of the Common Market. In spite of developments, half of the Danish population,

---

5 *Herren selv på Sions Bjerge for sit folk er skjold og værge.*
6 The first line of the song reads *Du danske Mand! Af al din Magt syng ud om vor gamle Mor!* [Thou Danish man, with all thy might, sing out about our old Mother [i.e. the homeland]].

not least those on the left wing – by contrast with today, where it is those on the right – with an elderly historian, Palle Lauring, and a young psychedelic poet, Ebbe Kløvedal, in the lead, proved to be more Danish than their parents or grandparents (who for the most part had never been outside Denmark's borders) had been in two world wars that had each threatened Denmark's existence as an independent state. Just as the national syndrome was about to die out, it had re-emerged; that ability seems to be one of Danish identity's most distinguishing features.

Carl Nielsen had not yet become 'The Dane' he was to become in the 1990s, but his Danishness had become an increasing problem for Danes. For although he was as great as the greatest – and besides was the only great composer Danish children got to know in school, not because he had written his great music, but because he had also written his little (Danish) songs – wasn't he also so quintessentially Danish that he did not have a real chance outside the Danish duck-pond? Was it now because we feared that he was not really so good that others could also take delight in him? Or was it rather that we wanted to have him for ourselves and did not want to part with him or risk being forced to change our perception of him?

We had had some help from a world-famous American, thus demonstrating our internationalism in opposition to provincialism. Leonard Bernstein had been in Copenhagen for the composer's centenary in 1965, had performed the *Sinfonia espansiva*, rubbed off the edges, inflated him into a fat romantic, so that every Dane who knew a little about classical music could hear that he was just as good as Dvořák or Brahms. This reassured the Danes, or the small sector of them that made up the musical public of the time; at last they could hear how great he was and feel convinced. The belt held, although this kind of treatment represented a reduction of his musical personality, sanctioned by international celebrity.

Anyone could say to themselves – but they didn't – that the cloud of Danish incense surrounding their composer would have to blow away sooner or later. The old who had dragged his legacy around with them, who had their roots in or close to the composer's own time, were dying out. Danes were also, like civilised people in many other parts of the world, in the process of hastily exploiting the countryside, building little detached houses, roads, factories and institutions, destroying nature and agriculture, at the rate of 30 to 40 hectares a day for decades, not to mention the transformation of the remaining agriculture. It became harder and harder to sing 'I know a larks' nest'. It was no longer to be taken for granted that children would have seen a lark, never mind its nest, which a few decades earlier we had learned to take care not to tread on. The song composer's image of Denmark was rapidly changing.

Then after decades of waiting there finally appeared in 1991 a new book about this composer, entitled *Carl Nielsen, the Dane*.[7] The 'little great Dane' the man was now

---

7 Jørgen I. Jensen, *Carl Nielsen – Danskeren*, Copenhagen 1991.

called on every page; now he was not only the composer of *Thou Danish Man* but the very incarnation of Thou Danish Man. But here it is time to get off the Danish wave and go back to find one of its points of origin: *Thou Danish Man* and its appearance 100 years ago.

1906 was not only the year of the premiere of the opera *Maskarade*, for the most part composed the previous year, which both proclaimed and made an issue of democratisation and equality; it was also the year in which the patriotic song *Thou Danish Man* was composed, performed and published (see *Fig. 2*), and began its triumphant sweep through Danish song and choral societies, thereby coming to represent the definitive breakthrough to the public at large for the high-culture composer.

There was a good deal of national incense in the air that year, not only in Denmark (where Christian IX, who had been King since 1863, died, and Frederik VIII was proclaimed King from the balcony on Amalienborg[8]), but also in Norway and Sweden, which had been united until Norway became independent the previous year.

In Denmark it had happened that when the assembled crowd on the Amalienborg courtyard on 30 January was due to break into song after the new King had been proclaimed, they divided into two groups. Some sang *Kong Christian* (King Christian), even though the king was now called Frederik, while others broke into *Det er et yndigt Land* (There is a beautiful country), perhaps because the king was no longer called Christian. The episode did not become an inspiration for Charles Ives, who had enough to do with musical collisions in public spaces in America; but it did unleash a great debate in the Danish papers about our patriotic songs. Among those who took part was Professor Vilhelm Andersen,[9] the librettist of *Maskarade*, but not Carl Nielsen – at least not directly.

In Norway and Sweden the dissolution of the union had set national impulses free, not only in Norway which could finally enrol in the company of nation states, but also in Sweden, which now experienced its geographical reduction, just as Denmark had in 1864.[10] It was symptomatic that in 1905 Wilhelm Stenhammar wrote and premiered his cantata *One People* (Ett Folk), in which he composed the national hymn 'Sweden, Sweden, Sweden, our native land, / place of our longing, our home on earth!.[11]

In 1906 for the first time a special Swedish music festival was held in Stockholm, at the end of May and the beginning of June. Nielsen was staying in Stockholm, and not only arranged contact with *Politiken*, which sent a correspondent, but also himself wrote an article about the music festival for the same paper. Here he dealt

---

8   The residence of the royal family in Copenhagen.

9   'Vore Nationalsange' [Our National Songs], *Politiken*, 4.3.1906.

10 Following military defeat at the hands of Prussia.

11 'Sverige, Sverige, Sverige fosterland, / vår längtans bygd, vårt hem på jorden!'

with the national idea, and since *Thou Danish Man* must have been composed at the same time or immediately after the article, it may not be entirely irrelevant to see what the composer wrote on this occasion:

> There is therefore a danger for art in the national element, and the more this quality is conscious, the greater the danger.
>
> As soon as one begins to finger and paw lasciviously at this gentle creature, good and healthy art has had it. The national element must warm, colour and as it were breathe its spirit into art, but it dare not in any way become its Alpha and Omega. So it was very disappointing to read the invitation in the Danish press a little while ago to take part in a competition for an overture along the lines of earlier works of this kind. It is quite incomprehensible that this invitation should have come from an excellent musician, and moreover a creative artist. The recipe for such a work would probably go roughly as follows: take one part Andantino in six-eight metre, one part minor mode and one part Danish stewed pears marinated overnight; stir well together, place over a gentle flame and simmer for approx. 20 minutes, and so on. But joking aside. What I mean is this: set no store by false piety, but only by good art. The national tone will come about of its own accord; indeed it is something we can hardly deny, even if we wanted to.[12]

The competition Nielsen refers to was arranged by the Danish Concert Society on the initiative of the returned émigré Dane, Asger Hamerik, and the prize of 1.000 kroner was shared between the composers Ludolf Nielsen and Joachim Bruun de Neergaard, for works that not a single person knows today. No, Nielsen did not enter the competition with his *Maskarade* Overture, and not only because it had not yet been composed but was only done at the last moment for the premiere in November. In any case it would hardly have been received as truly Danish, even though curiously enough *Maskarade* has since been described more than once as a Danish national opera!

In the first full biography of Nielsen there is a story about the origins of *Thou Danish Man*.[13] Its point is that Nielsen composed the melody without knowing the text. The story cannot be entirely substantiated from the existing sources, but neither is it contradicted by them. With this story as a starting-point, and supplemented by other sources, the following picture can be assembled:

---

12 'Svensk Musikfest' [Swedish Music Festival], *Politiken* 14.6.1906, reproduced in John Fellow (ed.), *Carl Nielsen til sin samtid*, Copenhagen 1999, 89.
13 Torben Meyer & Frede Schandorf Petersen, *Carl Nielsen, Kunstneren og Mennesket*, Copenhagen 1947-48, vol. 1, 286-287.

In 1906 the music hall writers Anton Melbye and Johannes Dam had decided to create an alternative show for Tivoli, which they called *The Summer Journey, a Copenhagen Vaudeville* (Sommerrejsen, en Kjøbenhavner-Vaudeville). In years to come it continued to play in the Tivoli Theatre, under the same title but with new musical numbers. The music was supplied by Olfert Jespersen, the cafe musician and composer of popular music, who as a young man had met Carl Nielsen in Odense, had been a guest in his little digs and had played there with him the violin sonata which the young military musician had composed, whereupon he had immediately recognised Nielsen's genius and had pushed to get him to Copenhagen and the world of great music. That had been the beginning of a lifelong friendship; Jespersen died shortly after Nielsen.

Olfert Jespersen's memoirs also tell us about *Thou Danish Man*, but he mixes up his own satirical patriotic song, *In little sea-encircled Radadulistan* (I det lille havomkranste Radadulistan), which does not come from the 1906 first version of *The Summer Journey*, together with *Thou Danish Man*, which indeed – rather like a draft for the little sea-encirled Radadulistan! – includes the line 'a circle of sea and fjord was laid around the house...'.[14] That makes him useless as a source, even though Nielsen's preface to the memoirs calls the book 'truthful as rust-free steel'.[15] The only trustworthy thing in Olfert Jespersen's report is probably the fact that he had nothing to do with *Thou Danish Man*, but that, as he writes, it was 'a kind of secretiveness that the authors of the text intended'.[16]

One day Melbye and Drachmann had been together in a cafe, according to *Politiken*. They had been talking about the issue of national song, which was much in the air at the time, and Melbye said to Drachmann: 'Well, after all you should write us the new patriotic Fatherland song!' 'If only I had the opportunity,' replied the bard. 'Aha, an opportunity,' said Melbye. 'If you really want an opportunity, then I'm writing a play at the moment, and I could certainly use a patriotic song there; there's your opportunity!'[17]

Drachmann was 60 that year, and the occasion was to be marked by a ceremonial performance at The Royal Theatre. Nielsen was engaged to write the music to the play *Sir Oluf, he rides–* (Hr. Oluf han rider–), which Drachmann was working on for the occasion. It ended up being a hectic time, with concurrent rehearsals for both *Maskarade* and *Sir Oluf*, which was to have its premiere a month before that of *Maskarade* on 11 November. *Sir Oluf* was to be one of Nielsen's most extended scores, though not a success; but that is another story.

Just as the collaboration between poet and composer was about to begin, Drachmann appeared one day in June, so the biography tells us, and invited Nielsen

---

14 *En krans af hav og fjord blev lagt om huset ...*

15 *Sandfærdig som rustfrit Staal.*

16 Olfert Jespersen, *Oplevelser* [Experiences], Copenhagen 1930, 127.

17 *Politiken*, 28.6.1906.

for lunch at the Langelinie Pavilion. 'When they were waiting for their coffee,' the story goes, 'and countless funny stories had seasoned the meal, Drachmann said "Nielsen, let's make a damned fatherland song!" On the menu he drew up a "mask"-verse, beginning with the nonsense lines:

> A man was walking across Vesterbro[18]
> He had a red skullcap on ...

Before they parted Nielsen was humming the melody to himself. And that is how *Thou Danish Man* came into the world.'[19]

On 26 June at 21.45 the premiere of *A Summer Journey* took place in Tivoli's Theatre Hall, and the names of Holger Drachmann and Carl Nielsen were not on the poster.

'It was like a Revue premiere, but without the Revue,' wrote *Nationaltidende* the next day. 'All the well-known faces, row upon row in the stalls – the whole pure-Copenhagen rose-bed .' Whether poet and composer also adorned the bed, the story does not tell. The patriotic fatherland song was the first number in the show.

> It began as a proper vaudeville in the old style, right down to a proper father-land song, which insofar as one could hear the text, was really beautiful. We are on an American steamship, which one evening is sweeping past the gentle Zealand coastline, and we get to know a stout butcher lady, who has fallen in love with an actor returning home from an American tour, and her two daughters, who have attached themselves to a tenor and a lay-preacher. At some moments there is a real atmosphere, at others we are entertained by deftly invented tricks. And when the act ends, with the help of a movable backdrop – which will create a perfect illusion when the machinery works better – by giving us a changing view over the straits,[20] there is real excitement in the audience.[21]

It was Henry Seemann in the role of engineer Carsten Holst, the returning émigré, who sang *Thou Danish Man* . *Politiken* wrote in its review that he 'sang as meltingly and believably as only a young, honest, Danish road-maker with full beard, trusting spaniel eyes and loose cuffs could do.' The ladies contributed to enhancing the mood: 'Miss Jutta Lund and Mrs Buemann swelled in competition, so that one's heart warmed on their behalf, and the latter appeared at some points in a Spanish costume, which certainly

---

18 Part of central Copenhagen; literal translation: "Western Town Gate".
19 Meyer & Schandorf Petersen, *op. cit.*, 286.
20 The Øresund: the straits separating Zealand from the southern Swedish province of Skåne.
21 *Nationaltidende*, 27.6.1906.

represented the far limits of daring for Tivoli, which is to say not so overwhelming, even though the little lady had neglected to do herself up at the back.'[22]

It was Miss Jutta Lund in the role of the butcher's widow Caroline Lassen, who after the patriotic song performed her song about *Poor Lassen* (Salig Lassen) – in waltz time, with music by Olfert Jespersen and text by Anton Melbye and/or Johannes Dam. The first verse went:

> Poor Lassen really was a good man,
> Nor was he disappointed in me,
> Yes, but to love a dead husband,
> No, I'm damned if I will.
> Ah, but think, what he said a few minutes before
> His soul flew up to heaven:
> Line [i.e. Caroline], before I die,
> Listen well now,
> I'm damned well asking you:
> Not to re-marry.
> My God, I obeyed my husband oh so often,
> But God knows, the dead can go too far,
> Shall you now, poor widow, be a wallflower?
> Not on your life, Lassen!
> My God, I obeyed my husband all too often,
> But God knows, the dead can go too far,
> Shall you now, poor widow, be a wallflower?
> Not on your life, my friend!

Two days later several Copenhagen newspapers revealed who the creators of *Thou Danish Man* were. The whole thing has the look of a certain calculation on the part of Tivoli and the authors of the revue. Then not many days went past before the question arose of publishing the song separately. Anton Melbye wrote to Nielsen on a Sunday shortly after the premiere – which would make the date in all probability 1 July 1906:

> My dear composer!
> Thank you for the song – I would have thanked you more effusively, had it been heard to better advantage that evening, but tenors and block-heads seem nine out of ten times to be one and the same. Be that as it may (as it happens the song is more and more of a success every evening, and it may well be that

---

22 *Politiken*, 27.6.1906.

it will become something like what we were aiming for, even though Drach-mann didn't find the right words) I am in no doubt that the melody is first-rate and will carry the song aloft.

Of course you won't have anything against the song's appearing with your music in a special edition from Wilhelm Hansen, will you? Wouldn't it be an idea for your wife to design a front cover, so that we can avoid the terri-bly banal drawings Hansen so often comes up with.

Herewith the text. Please be so good as to get the song done as soon as possible.[23]

This seems to confirm that the story of Drachmann's "mask"-verse as the basis for Nielsen's melody has some foundation or other in reality; why else should Nielsen have had the text sent to him at this late stage? But the text that was enclosed with the letter has not survived. The surviving autograph in the Carl Nielsen Collection[24] – a printer's copy with corrections in Drachmann's hand to the text in the first and sec-ond verses – is undated, and in all probability it was prepared after the premiere and after Nielsen had received the text with Anton Melbye's Sunday letter. A surviving pencil draft is similarly undated (see *Fig. 1*),[25] but corrections in the underlaid text (for instance, '*Syng ud hver Dansk*' [Sing out, every Dane] corrected to '*Du danske Mand*') *may* indicate that the text was created for and adapted to the notes. Besides, the draft originally belonged to Henrik Knudsen,[26] who may also be supposed to be the source of the story about the origins of *Thou Danish Man* .

An undated manuscript of the text in Holger Drachmann's hand is also pre-served.[27] According to a note on the envelope it comes from Anton Melbye's widow, and it may be assumed to have been the basis both for the text that Henry Seemann sang at the performance and for the one that Melbye sent Nielsen with his Sunday letter. This manuscript must have come into being after Nielsen's sketch, which is the only source to disclose the variant opening words, and before the printer's copy, in which Drachmann made corrections in relation to his manuscript, as for example in the last line of the second verse: from '*Saa straaler Livets Friskhed som Frihedens lyse Skat*' (Thus shines the freshness of life, like the bright treasure of freedom) to the familiar '*Saa lyser Livets friskhed fra Frihedens dyre Skat*' (Thus the freshness of life is lit up by the precious treasure of freedom).

In the printer's copy Nielsen originally gave the third verse in accordance with the Drachmann manuscript we know, with the last three lines thus:

23 *DK-Kk*, CNA 1ab.
24 *DK-Kk*, CNS 130a.
25 *DK-Kk*, CNS 130d.
26 Cf. *DK-Kk*, CNS 254, K 1.
27 *DK-Kk*, NKS 2936 4°. My thanks to Elly Bruunshuus Petersen for drawing this manuscript to my attention.

If the farmer has tilled the land
Then he meets the water:
There the Danish sailor steadily keeps guard like a Viking[28]

Then he crossed out these lines and wrote the words we know:

And as the plough furrows the land,
So the keel plies the water.
Patiently the Danish sailor stands his Viking-Guard at the sea [29]

In Drachmann's manuscript, written in ink, the third verse is crossed out and re-written in its final version in pencil. In the printer's copy Drachmann signed Nielsen's correction of the last three lines, and it is hard not to conclude that these lines are the work of Nielsen, subsequently approved by Drachmann. Nielsen too, so it seems, felt that Drachmann had not 'found the right words', as Melbye wrote. There is some evidence that Henry Seemannn sang various versions of the text before it was finalised.

A letter from Melbye to Drachmann of 7 June may be the first eye-witness evidence of the process that led to *Thou Danish Man*. Melbye had just been visited by Nielsen, who had just returned from the Swedish Music Festival in Stockholm, and he asked Drachmann for a meeting of all three men the next day, 'in connection with the matter you probably know about'.[30] We do not know whether this meeting came to anything, whether Melbye's letter perhaps led to the above-mentioned lunch at the Langelinie Pavilion, or whether the facts are altogether otherwise. In any case, on 17 June a melody was composed for a song, whose title was *Du danske Mand*, and with which Melbye was apparently (still) not satisfied. For Nielsen wrote:

Dear Anton Melbye!
The conclusion of the melody cannot be otherwise, if it is going to make proper sense: but in case H.D. has another poem I dare say I can toss off a completely new one, perhaps also invent others [i.e. melodies] for *Thou Danish Man*, but I think as a whole the thing isn't so bad as it stands.
In haste, your

Carl Nielsen[31]

---

28 *Har Bonden pløjet Landet / Saa mødes han med Vandet: / Dèr ta'r den danske Sømand som Vikingen støt sin Vagt*
29 *Og furer Ploven Landet, / Saa skurer Kølen Vandet, / Støt staar den danske Sømand paa Havet sin Viking-Vagt*
30 *DK-Kk*, NKS 4653 4°.
31 *DK-Kk*, NKS 4619 4°, and Irmelin Eggert Møller & Torben Meyer, *Carl Nielsens breve*, Copenhagen 1954, 76.

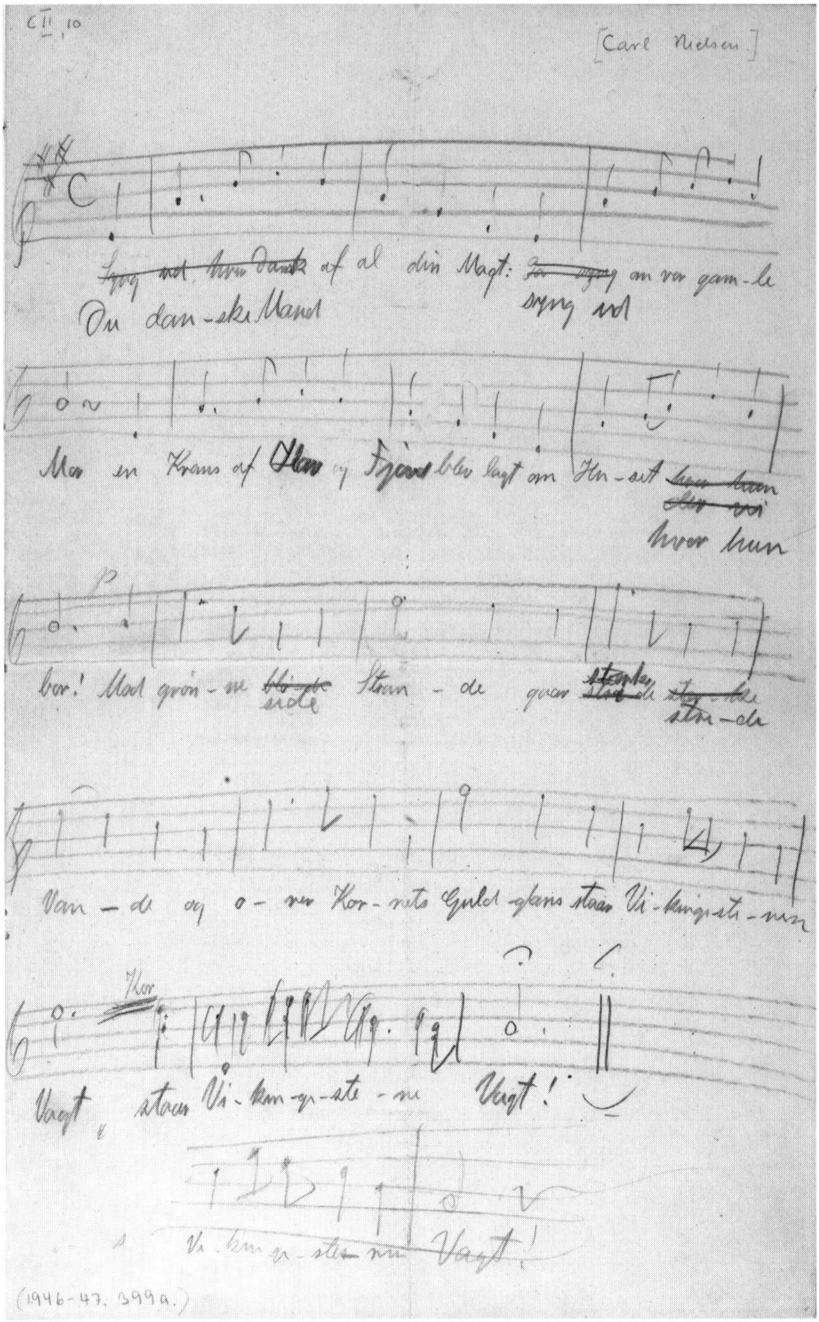

FIG. 1: *Nielsen's sketch of* Thou Danish Man. *The Royal Library, Copenhagen, CNS 130d*

FIG. 2: Song of the Fatherland. (*Fædrelandssang*). *Title page of the first edition from 1906 of Nielsen's song, "Thou Man of Denmark". See music and text on the following pages*

Fædrelandssang.

CARL NIELSEN.

Tempo giusto.

SANG.

PIANO.

mf

f

1. Du dan - ske Mand! af al din Magt syng ud om vor gam - le Mor! En Krans af Hav og Fjord blev lagt om Hu - set, hvor hun bor: Mod grøn - ne, si - de Stran - de gaar

Copyright 1906 by Wilhem Hansen, Kjøbenhavn & Leipzig.   13869

1940

3

2.

Syng ud— og Sorg fra Fortids Nat
Blir Smil paa hver Glædesdag,
Vor Himmel skifter Farve brat
Men aldrig Folkets Flag.
Som Danmarks blide Kvinder
Har røde-hvide Kinder
Saa lyser Livets Friskhed |: fra Frihedens dyre Skat. :|

3.

Vort gamle Land! af al vor Magt
Vi øger din Rigdoms Ring,
Gaar fremad seigt og uforsagt,
Om ej i store Spring.
Og furer Ploven Landet,
Saa skurer Kølen Vandet
Støt staar den danske Sømand |: paa Havet sin Viking-Vagt. :|

HOLGER DRACHMANN.

13869   Wilhelm Hansens Nodestik og Tryk, København.

Two months after the premiere of *The Summer Journey*, more precisely on 28 August 1906, Wilhelm Hansens Musikforlag announced the publication of Holger Drachmann's and Carl Nielsen's 'Patriotic Song' in *Politiken* and elsewhere. The song could now be purchased for 75 øre. In the same announcement, a piano score of extracts from Franz Lehár's *The Merry Widow* was advertised at 2 kroner. The operetta had been conquering the world since its premiere in Vienna on 30 December 1905, and ten days before Hansens' advertisement it had been staged in Copenhagen, on 18 August at the Casino Theatre, where Lehár himself conducted. Later that same year Nielsen said laconically in a lecture that there could be no comparison between 18th-century composers and luminaries of the day – 'not even excepting the composer of *The Merry Widow*'.[32]

Thou Danish Man also appeared in an edition for mixed choir, arranged by the composer, in the coming years becoming standard repertoire in most Danish choral societies, and we may safely say that the original circumstances were forgotten. In a curious way the song does, however, play a role in an episode retold seven years later by the actor Johannes Nielsen on the way to Oslo, in a letter from a Scandinavian-American Line steamship. The movable backdrop in the Tivoli revue is replaced by the real Danish landscape, and what was originally a return home is now a voyage away:

> Dear Carl!
> I'm on a lightning trip to Christiania [Oslo] by steamship. Just now (9 in the evening) I was standing on deck and heard a flock of émigrés singing farewell to Denmark with remarkable, melancholy enthusiasm. Last and loudest they sang Carl Nielsen's *Du danske Mand*. That made me think of you and about the significance of good art as a binding force between human minds. So, my greetings to you this evening. I know that ten Danes – young and not so young on the way to meet their fate – have said farewell to the past in tones that first sounded in your – dare I say it? – heart. Mine was glad to hear it. The whole thing was so artless and beautiful. At two o'clock when we were sailing along , tears ran down their cheeks; now their pains fade away in simple harmonies – a farewell in which gratitude shines and which awakens strength and hope – kind, good folk, the West Jutlanders. I wanted to chat to them, but they were taciturn and drew back. I hope it amuses you to hear that you gave their feelings a good course to follow.
> > Greetings to you and yours!
> > Yours sincerely
> > Johannes[33]

32 John Fellow (ed.), *Carl Nielsen til sin samtid*, Copenhagen 1999, 60.
33 *DK-Kk* , CNA 1Ab, Johannes Nielsen to Carl Nielsen 20.2.1913.

After Nielsen's death *Thou Danish Man* was daily fare in Danish folk high schools and public primary schools[34] and everywhere where there was mass singing. During the Nazi occupation it also became part of a general version of mass singing (the so-called "alsang"), and when Einar Nørby made his famous recording on 26 October 1943, it was during the rescue operation for Danish Jews, which marked the move among the Danish population towards support for the line of resistance. The closing lines, 'Steadily the Danish sailor stands his Viking-Guard at sea' then made *Thou Danish Man* into a song of struggle and mobilisation.

We can conclude: When those of us who were only born after the Second World War – after the culmination and eventual defeat of nationalist hysteria, as we believed at that time – ironically bawled out *Thou Danish Man* in Danish schools in the late 1950s and early 60s, we were, without realising it, in closer contact with the song's original context than our elders had been, for whom the song had been a serious matter and for whom it meant so much.

Thou Danish Man came into being as a result of the *Maskarade* pranks; it could have been sung by Henrik in the opera! Of course we could not have guessed that. We knew *Thou Danish Man* and the other songs before we got to know the opera – if we ever did get to know it; for most of us the slide into the world of commercial West-European music intervened. The bawling of the song was combined with a certain delightful feeling of guilt and for me it was a revelation many years later to discover the true – ironic – context of the story and the song.

The transformation process of *Thou Danish Man* began already with its publication. It was not Anne Marie Carl-Nielsen who designed the cover, as Anton Melbye had suggested it should be. Instead it was provided with an ordinary – Danish – picture by Hans Nicolai Hansen: in the foreground was the corner of a cornfield and a grave from olden days, in the middle a farmer's and a fisherman's house and two large windblown trees. How this illustration came about, and whether there was any conflict involved, we do not know, but there certainly is a story to tell concerning a similar matter:

In 1924, eighteen years after *Thou Danish Man*, Nielsen edited *Melodies for the Songbook "Denmark"* for Wilhelm Hansens Forlag.[35] From the surviving correspondence we can see that he himself thought that he and the publishers had an agreement that he and wood-engraver Frederik Hendriksen could decide how the title page should look. Joakim Skovgaard was considered for the job, but he did not have

---

34 The folk high schools ("Folkehøjskoler") were based on the ideas of N.F.S. Grundtvig, originally attracting farmers' sons and daughters in their teens and twenties. The teaching was based on what Grundtvig called "the living word", concentrated on Danish history and literature. It was Grundtvig's way of enlightening the Danish rural population.
35 Carl Nielsen & Hakon Andersen *Melodier til Sangbogen "Danmark"*, Copenhagen 1924.

time, and Nielsen therefore got his daughter Anne Marie Telmányi (known as Søs) to make some sketches, including singing children's heads for the front, and for the reverse a cupid riding on the back of a singing lark. Nielsen and Hendriksen were both happy with this proposal.

But the publishers were not. For such a songbook they wanted a *Danish* motif, 'something along the lines of *The Ploughman*,[36] for example', and they proposed the illustrator Kristian Kongstad. That suggestion provoked the following characteristic piece of prose from Nielsen:

> This songbook was interesting for me to produce, and I want it to appear both externally and internally in an artistic spirit. So far as the title-page is concerned, I cannot permit that a fourth-rate artist (as has been named) should produce it. I prefer an artistic hand over a nice and smooth but meaningless drawing. I would remind you that my Chaconne, [Theme and] Variations and Second [Violin] Sonata are only provided with the simple letters, in modest by no means poor taste. That is far preferable to pictures and drawings when they show no talent. In the world of books as a rule a certain traditional culture has been retained, but if we look at music shop-windows all over Europe, what we have to put up with is so hideous, stupid, tasteless and surpassingly nonsensical, that it beggars description. Since my early youth I have mixed with visual artists more than with musicians (my friends include the painters Tuxen, the Anchers, Willumsen, [Johannes] Kragh, Karl Madsen and others), so Hr. Asger Wilhelm Hansen can probably rest assured and keep to the agreement, namely that I, together with Hr. Hendriksen and some artist or other, can sort this little matter out.[37]

But the publishers dug their heels in. Then Nielsen declared that he could not 'prevent the firm from going back on its agreement and making a new title page. But I hereby inform you that the songbook cannot be published for the present, since I shall at least have to withdraw my new melodies and replace them with other existing ones.'[38]

The firm answered that they had approached Joakim Skovgaard in connection with the design of the title page, and that they intended to bring out the songbook in accordance with the contract of 11 April. What then transpired between the parties, the surviving correspondence does not reveal, but Skovgaard presumably still did not have time, or else he did not want to get embroiled in such an inflammatory situa-

---

36 Famous painting by Peter Hansen (1868-1928), one of the 'Funen Painters'.
37 Carl Nielsen to Wilhelm Hansen 27.6.1924 (*DK-Kk*, Wilhelm Hansen Archive).
38 Carl Nielsen to Wilhelm Hansen 6.8.1924 (*DK-Kk*, Wilhelm Hansen Archive).

tion, and six days later the publishers informed the composer, who was staying in Skagen, that they had that same day 'written to Søs and invited her to draw a title with a Danish motif for the Collection of *Melodies for the Songbook "Denmark"*'.

For those Danes old enough to have forgotten it, and those younger ones who have never had the *Collection of Melodies for the Songbook 'Denmark'* in their hands: the drawing on the title page shows a Danish landscape with the sun rising over the horizon, and in the foreground a farmer with a plough drawn by two energetic horses: in other words a proper Danish ploughman, drawn not by the fourth-rate artist named, but by Anne Marie Telmányi, i.e. by artistic, yet tied hands! And the moral of the story: even the greatest are powerless against the spirit of the times.

With *Thou Danish Man* something happened with Nielsen's relationship to his target group, to put it in modern terms. He, who came neither from the upper class, nor from the middle class or the culture-bearing strata in the large towns, but who from the beginning had striven towards the 'great music' that sought its public especially in these circles, had suddenly in a short space of time experienced that he was in a position to write music that appealed to the broader layer of society. In the next few years it happened yet again, with *John the Roadman*, and while we may perhaps dispute the value – at any rate the degree of patriotic seriousness – in *Thou Danish Man*, there is no gainsaying the artistic and social seriousness in *John the Roadman*.

Jeppe Aakjær's poem was first published in *Politiken* on 27 June 1905. We know from Nielsen's diary that he composed the melody for it almost exactly two years later, on 25 June 1907. He did not hit on the melody as easily as he had in the case of *Thou Danish Man*, and here the text was to a marked degree the starting point and source of inspiration. In an interview from 1918 he himself related:

> And often for me a great deal of work goes into a little thing. For example, the melody to 'Jens Vejmand' cost me many – probably more than 50 – vain attempts in the course of three to four months; I felt that all the melodies I invented were too artificial, and I had actually put the poem out of my thoughts. But then one fine day the melody appeared by itself – when I was about to catch the train to Klampenborg – and then it was written down in the course of a few minutes.[39]

The same year it appeared in the collection entitled *Strofiske Sange*, Op. 21, and it by no means turned out to be an immediate hit. But two years later one of the day's

---

39 Fellow, *op. cit.*, 226.

greatest and most popular tenors, Vilhelm Herold, who was fortunately Danish, took *John the Roadman* into his repertoire, and he recorded it on gramophone records, a very new and very scratchy medium at the time.

'It was like an epidemic', as Nielsen himself put it. On a train journey across Funen, together with his family and in the company of author Jakob Knudsen and his brother Lars Knudsen (who had created the role of Arv in *Maskarade*), he witnessed his fellow-travellers singing and playing *John the Roadman*. Nielsen's wife, the sculptress, said to a man who was playing the mouth organ: 'How can you bear to play that terrible melody?', but the other travellers, who clearly did not know who was with them, got cross, and the man growled: 'It's *not* terrible!'[40]

'It really seems to be as though the whole population is singing this song', Nielsen wrote in his diary after that experience.[41] But *John the Roadman* – not only the man but also the song about him – was also mistreated. Walking one day from Frederiksholms Kanal to Islands Brygge Nielsen one day heard 'five barrel organs performing 'Jens Vejmand' in *waltz-time*',[42] and in 1910 a Copenhagen 'Gramophone orchestra' recorded a polka arrangement of the song.

The other smash hit that year was Anton Melbye's and Berniaux's *Jeannette i den grønne Skov* (Jeannette in the Green Wood); now Nielsen was no longer collaborating with Melbye – they had become competitors! One day when Nielsen was visiting the Parliament building (his brother Valdemar was for a short time Member of Parliament for the *Radikal* Party), 'an honourable member over from Jutland' said to him: 'Listen, you're a musician, can't you tell us which melody is worse, 'Jens Vejmand' or 'Jeanette i den grønne Skov'; they're both ugly melodies. He did not know that I was to blame for 'Jens Vejmand', and my opinion of the melody was of course rather different from his', Nielsen commented.[43]

Thou Danish Man and *John the Roadman* each in its own way showed Nielsen that he had the chance to speak to a larger public, and also to go beyond the boundaries of concert music. This experience precedes his work on reforming the *folkelige*[44] song, which he threw himself into for the rest of his life, side-by-side with his high-art music. Others in this situation would perhaps have thought of financial gain and would have switched to composing hit songs and tunes. But it was not money that Nielsen was after. 'I advise youngsters not to become artists, because it's impossible to make a living at it in this country, unless you have luck with a foxtrot or something like that', he observed at the height of his fame in 1926, adding that he had received

40 Fellow, *op. cit*, 295.
41 Diary entry of 6.7.1910 (*DK-Kk*, CNA IC). Cf. John Fellow (ed.), *Carl Nielsen Brevudgaven*, Copenhagen 2007, vol.3, 865.
42 Fellow (1999), *op. cit.*, 295.
43 *Ibid*.
44 See introductory note of Vorre's and Vestergaard's article, p. 80.

only 50 kroner for *John the Roadman* once and for all![45] Shortly before that, Jacob Gade's *Tango Jalousie* had begun its worldwide conquest, and gold had begun to pour in for a quite different type of composer.

Nielsen did not formulate either his theory and aesthetics of music or his artistic philosophy directly; he lived and practised them all together – and said a good deal about them on various occasions. To the social democratic politician A.C. Meyer he wrote for example in 1918: 'Recently I have given lectures about the Original and Simple in music, and I pointed out precisely that without going back to the easily understandable in art, music – including the higher art-music – has lost its way and has sacrificed its importance as a means of education for the people.'[46] In the lecture in question, which he gave several times in 1917 and 1918, he also bracketed, without actually making art into religion, the great artists with the founders of religion: 'At a certain moment they had a visionary sensation: a state of ecstasy, a feeling of infinite joy, an indescribable feeling of power'. And those who know nothing of the kind he advised in no uncertain terms to 'put art aside and become good everyday people'.[47]

An art that is a means of education for the people; artists under the obligation of a fundamental experience that bears comparison with the founders of religions! Evidently what drove Nielsen was neither his own time's notions of art and culture nor our own. And if he could say: 'We are living in a time when spiritual life for the most part is superficial',[48] what would he have said about our own time? Nielsen's artistic standpoints resemble those of antiquity more than they do ours, and if we only confront him and his work with our own contemporary questions, then we have written off in advance any chance of understanding his essence.

His output of songs, which in the earlier cycles began as 'higher art-music', developed into a pedagogic project that made use of strophic songs. His experience with the revue-vaudeville-patriotic-song *Thou Danish Man* must have been decisive for that development. The songs were called Danish songs in their day; they naturally set Danish texts – German songs could hardly have served his pedagogic aims. Some of the song texts also make use of a nationalist vocabulary that can seem to go against the composer's many critical declarations down the years about the 'national'. An investigation into the matter, however, demands more than a weighing of the content of a selection of the song texts, made from the point of view of today's understanding of the national, or the nationalistic, as university jargon now quite unhistorically has it.

45 Fellow (1999), *op. cit.*, 385.
46 *DK-Kk*, CNA, Carl Nielsen to A.C. Meyer 23.2.1918. Cf. Eggert Møller & Meyer, *op. cit.*, 171.
47 Fellow (1999), *op. cit*, 214.
48 Fellow (1999), *op. cit.*, 213.

In opposition to the Second Viennese School, who for years consciously chose to shut themselves away in a private society, away from a public they in any case did not have, Nielsen's cultural premises were 'softer'. In Denmark there was a living folk tradition, with its starting point in Grundtvig and the folk high school movement, and Nielsen himself as a child had experienced a spiritual awakening on his home ground, via his encounter with Klaus Berntsen and with that movement. There is nothing to indicate that he endorsed the substance in the folk high schools' curriculum uncritically, but to the last he talked positively about its pedagogic, educational power, and with his output of songs he sought to influence musical development directly and from the bottom up. In this way he was crucial.

The national incense belonged to that time. In Denmark (then) it represented not an aggressive nationalism, but a threatened country's attempt to hold its head high. For another time and another attitude, also for mine, the national incense may seem bogus and tasteless, but that does not mean that every nature- or folk-life picture from the Danish past is an instance of nationalism. Whether Nielsen contributed to making the music of his time more or less national can only be answered if the field of investigation is widened to include also the lesser and forgotten spirits, and the period as a whole. The question is surely also to what degree it was the composer's times that drew *him* more in a national direction? The example of the beginning with *Thou Danish Man* is striking. Nielsen's position, and the Danish tradition, which allowed him at one and the same time to be a humanist-utopian and a day-to-day practitioner in music great and small, meant of course that he ran the risk of getting his fingers burnt. That he was able to make use of the special Danish circumstances in an attempt to bind culture together from top to bottom did not make him especially Danish; at the end of the day it perhaps provided him with rather more favourable conditions for being universal.

The motives behind the individual songs may be very different – witness *Thou Danish Man* and *John the Roadman*! – and hard to discern. Both for Nielsen's psalms and for many of his songs, it seems that his attitude to the text was not always as decisive as his attitude to an existing and widely disseminated, bad melody, which needed to be replaced. In many cases it was others who chose the texts for him: for some of the songs Thomas Laub, for the psalms Valdemar Brücker. Many of the best-known songs have their origins in theatre music and occasional works, whose texts the composer did not know when he agreed to write the music. He wrote music to other texts on the basis of personal acquaintance with the authors. The motives are manifold, and *Du danske Mand* is not the first song whose history places it in another light. In the case of *Danmark i tusind Aar* (Denmark for a thousand years), the secular concluding chorale to the 1917 *Cantata for the Society of Wholesalers*, Valdemar Rørdam wrote the words to a melody that Nielsen had written the year before for the Shakespeare celebration at Kronborg,[49] and it was not incorporated into the folk high school tradition by Nielsen himself, but was only included in 1940, following the German occupation of Denmark, during which it came to play a role in the alsang-movement – and after the war in the school singing classes, even though the author of the text had during the war not exactly taken the part of a good Dane![50]

As for Nielsen – and his time and afterwards – we cannot know too much if we want to avoid barking up the wrong tree. Let that be yet another argument for doing all the massive source-work with notes and texts, for both the main works and the occasional ones, the writings, the letters and the documents. The more we know, the better the questions we can address both to the past and to the present. Art and scholarship, indeed every work of the human soul, presumes the ability and the will to rise above the endless carousel of the spirit of the age, not the ability to read the way the wind is blowing or the inclination to surrender to one's own times.

Translated by David Fanning

A B S T R A C T

From his starting point in the instrumental music of his native Funen, Nielsen aspired towards the world of great art music, placing himself in the continuation of the classical central European tradition. In the first decade of the new century, two of his songs became national treasures, *landeplager* – i.e. 'all the rage', or 'hits' as later generations would have called them. He composed the first one, *Thou Danish Man* (Du danske Mand), as an ironic song for a music hall show, and without knowledge of the text. Even so the song was received as a manifestation of the Danish national spirit, which continued to be the case as late as the mobilisation of public opinion against the German occupation of Denmark in the Second World War. From the composer's point of view these songs showed first and foremost that he was able to reach a wider public, and they formed the background for the pedagogic project (not National but *folkeligt*, i.e. Popular, in spirit) that he developed for the rest of his life through his song output, running side by side with his 'great' works.

49 The setting for *Hamlet*, at Helsingør (Elsinore) on the north-east coast of Zealand.

50 Valdemar Rørdam, Danish poet (1872-1946). During the German occupation Rørdam praised the German attack on The Soviet Union, and after the War he was excluded from the Danish Society of Authors because of "non-national attitudes".

THE ROSENHOFF AFFAIR

By Lisbeth Ahlgren Jensen

Of all the teachers at Copenhagen's Conservatory of Music it was undoubtedly Orla Rosenhoff (1844-1905) who was of the greatest significance for Nielsen.[1] Nielsen acknowledged this in dedicating his first major choral work, *Hymnus amoris*, to Rosenhoff in 1896 and also in various statements about his teacher's professional and human qualities, as for example in an interview in 1894:

> In passionate, enthusiastically streaming words, Nielsen tells of his extraordinary indebtedness to Rosenhoff – the outstanding teacher and fine human being, but also excessively modest, gifted musician, who a few years ago was thrown out of the Conservatory in the most shameful manner. 'That wretched institution', Nielsen quivers, clenching his teeth and his fists.[2]

The assertion about Rosenhoff's 'shameful' dismissal from the Conservatory is immediately remarkable. How could it come about that such a highly respected teacher could be 'thrown out of the Conservatory?' What was behind it? And what was the significance of his treatment in this way? These are some of the questions that this article seeks to answer. The aim is on the one hand to give an insight into theory and composition teaching at the Conservatory of Music during and immediately after Nielsen's studies, and on the other hand to investigate what kind of reputation the Conservatory had at the time. Both Nielsen's declaration about 'that wretched institution' and the coverage of the Rosenhoff affair in the press may give us cause to shake up the time-honoured view of the Conservatory of Music as an indisputable stronghold of musical education. Even when this valuation is not explicitly voiced, it underpins many an account, and it therefore functions as a point of orientation for evaluating the development of Danish musical culture. Nevertheless it is not my in-

---

1 K(j)øbenhavns Musikkonservatorium (The Copenhagen Conservatory of Music) was founded in 1867 as a private institution; later it became the leading musical college under its present name Det Kongelige Danske Musikkonservatorium (The Royal Danish Conservatory of Music).
2 Interview with Charles Kjerulf, *Politiken* 14.3.1894

tention in this article to condemn the Conservatory's fickle policies, as they appear to be in the last decade of the nineteenth century, when there was a power vacuum after Niels Gade's death. Irrespective of whether Rosenhoff's dismissal was based on a misunderstanding or was the result of a deliberate educational and personnel policy decision, it had immediate consequences, both on the personal and institutional level, and there is therefore good reason to go into the 'Rosenhoff affair',[3] as it was dubbed in the daily papers. It is my conviction that the circumstances of Rosenhoff's removal may be seen as an example of how Danish cultural politics – at least in the field of music – in some cases rest as much on coincidences or on faulty decisions as on the well-considered resolutions of wise men.

The Rosenhoff affair occurred in 1892, when Copenhagen's Conservatory of Music was celebrating its 25th anniversary, and the coincidence of the two events presumably contributed to the fact that Rosenhoff's dismissal was more in the public eye than if it had taken place at another point in time. But the very fact that it was linked with such an otherwise favourable circumstance as the celebration of a jubilee also has the effect that the Conservatory's reputation at the time can be illuminated in a more nuanced manner than if the jubilee had merely been praised in panegyric phrases.

As an introduction I shall illustrate press coverage of the matter; then I shall seek to pin down what Orla Rosenhoff stood for as a teacher; finally I shall attempt to place the Conservatory's decision to dismiss him in the context of the place that music theory subsequently acquired in music education.

Press Coverage of the Rosenhoff Affair

The matter of Rosenhoff's dismissal was first made public knowledge in an article in the daily paper *København* on 17 February 1892, under the heading 'The Conservatory of Music and Mr. O. Rosenhoff'. The sequence of events may be broadly described as follows: approximately a year after Gade's death, Rosenhoff asked the Board of Directors of the Conservatory for permission to guide his pupils right through to their final exams, instead of merely giving them elementary instruction in theory. In Rosenhoff's opinion, this would mean formalising a practice that had existed with the Board's approval for several years. The Board seemed at first to be positively inclined towards Rosenhoff's recommendation, but it asked him to submit a written request. This was done, but since Rosenhoff regarded it as a formality, he did not do to any great trouble over his request, though he did underline that he would leave the Conservatory if it was not approved. His surprise was therefore all the greater when after the Christmas 1891-92 vacation he presented himself for the new academic year

---

3 *København* 26.2.1892.

and learned that the Board's refusal was in the post. Thus, in reality Rosenhoff was sacked because the Board wished to continue the previous arrangements for theory instruction and had therefore not accepted his request.

Rosenhoff's threat to resign was therefore either not taken seriously or seen as a welcome opportunity to get rid of him, unless the dismissal was actually an unforeseen turn of events.

Press coverage was not confined to articles *about* Rosenhoff's dismissal, but also included contributions from the parties involved, which is to say from Rosenhoff himself and from the Board of the Conservatory. In addition there were consequences in the form of a report from Rosenhoff to the Ministry of Culture.[4] So the affair can be illustrated with many written statements, and curiously enough they are amazingly uniform so far as the substance of the matter is concerned, but naturally they illustrate the matter from various points of view, depending on the interests of the protagonists.

Stimulated by the press attention, Rosenhoff himself wrote a lengthy article, which was printed in *Dagens Nyheder* on 25 February 1892. For the sake of thoroughness he chose an historic approach and retold how in 1881 he had been invited by Gade to take over instruction in harmony following on from Johan Christian Gebauer. At that time the subject was not in any great favour, he claimed, in that 'Discipline in the lessons was slack, and only few of the pupils were in the habit of preparing themselves for them, so that there was much to tackle.'[5] As a means of making the subject more rigorous, Rosenhoff persuaded Gade to introduce examinations in music theory, which not only had a beneficial effect on discipline but also, according to Rosenhoff, could be interpreted as an appreciation of his efforts. Having worked as a theory teacher for one year, he was additionally entrusted with the task of instructing some of the pupils in 'Music Theory's next discipline: counterpoint and fugue', which for the previous 14 years had been J.P.E. Hartmann's 'speciality'. According to Rosenhoff, that testified to the great significance of the subject, and he therefore felt himself further reassured that the Board of Directors appreciated his efforts:

> I venture to claim without immodesty, that the fact that both Gade and Hartmann (together with the third director, [Holger Simon] Paulli) trusted me to teach *independently* alongside Hartmann, shows that these men had the feeling that it would be unreasonable to confine me to the initial levels of music theory.[6]

---

4 Ministry for Church and Education. Office No. 3. Item No. 205/92. Rigsarkivet. Letter from Orla Rosenhoff, 23.3.1892.

5 *Dagens Nyheder* 25.2.1892. Rosenhoff's view is borne out in Angul Hammerich, *Kjøbenhavns Musikkonservatorium 1876-1892*, 1892, 35.

6 *Ibid.*

So the situation for many years had been that Rosenhoff 'led the instruction in harmony, counterpoint and fugue, for a large proportion of the Conservatory's pupils, while music theory's third field of discipline (form, in conjunction with instrumentation and music history) was Gade's responsibility'.[7]

However, since Gade could not manage to teach all the many pupils admitted by the Conservatory, he allowed Rosenhoff to give some of the most talented students exercises in free composition, and he gave him a free hand in that respect, which suited Rosenhoff very well: 'I used to the full the opportunity this provided to allow the students to make practical use of their theoretical knowledge.' Up to Gade's death in December 1890, Rosenhoff therefore enjoyed an 'untroubled and satisfying period of activity' at the Conservatory. However, after the death of the powerful Director, there should in his opinion have been discussion as to what should happen. Either 'Gade's position should have been considered a kind of place of honour', which could only be filled by a figure of comparable authority, or the classes should have been shared out among the suitable theory teachers. But neither of these things was done:

> They gave Gade's chair to Professor Otto Malling and thereby maintained the old order of teaching, with special teachers in harmony, counterpoint and composition – an arrangement which in itself is wholly unreasonable, and which so far as I know is unheard of at the best foreign Conservatories.

Although we may doubt whether Rosenhoff's point of view was as widely shared as he claimed, it is interesting to note how he viewed the relationship between theory and practice:

> The view has long since been accepted that the harmony teacher, right from the first stages of his teaching, should also function as a composition teacher, making practical use of the material taught, in parallel with its acquisition by the student, by means of free exercises. Accordingly it must always be arbitrary to want to introduce composition teaching as a special subject at a certain later point in time. Composition is there from the very first moment, and it continues to be there so long as studies continue. It relates to harmony roughly as written language exercises do to basic drills and grammar. But even apart from this illogicality of principle, it is important to recognise that it may always be disturbing for pedagogical consistency when the same teacher does not guide his students from the beginnings of the subject to the end.

---

7 *Ibid.*

So Rosenhoff compared the pedagogy of music theory with that of language, in which exercises in writing were practical tasks that gave the pupil the chance to try out what he had learned (and the teacher the chance to check that the material had been understood). That he gave the most talented students 'free exercises' and therefore encouraged them to take a *creative* attitude to music, shows also that he was an advocate for a special way of fostering talent. All in all Rosenhoff depicts himself as a teacher who placed the emphasis on giving his students craftsmanly foundations, and on continuity both in content and method between theory and practice, just as he found it essential to stimulate the most talented students. At first glance this may not exactly sound pedagogically ground-breaking, but at least one of his pupils – Carl Nielsen – perceived his pedagogy to be a welcome alternative to Gade's methods, of which he observed:

> In my third year at the Conservatory I had classes with Gade, but I cannot honestly say that I learned much in them. We were in a group of something like 14 or 15 students, and Gade told us a lot about Raphael, Charlemagne, Øhlenschläger and the like, but occasionally he also played for us, and that was always both beautiful and entertaining. However, the whole thing was fragmentary and remarkably incoherent, and since he frequently glanced at his beautiful gold watch, I understood that he had probably higher things on his mind and that he couldn't wait to get home to his own work.[8]

One gets an impression of the extent to which Gade's views on music differed from Rosenhoff's from a statement by another pupil at the Conservatory. To a question about how to compose 'beautiful' melodies Gade is supposed to have replied:

> Well, you see, that is actually a secret, namely inspiration – for 'all good gifts come from heaven above', and that creates both melody and harmony in our hearts. And then, well, then one composes. Therefore, my young friend, always remember that in order to create a composition you must first have an inspiration – a singing theme – which one then fashions again in harmony.[9]

According to this romantic way of thinking, which valued the *inspired* and the *intuitive* higher than the craftsmanly, it would seem almost superfluous to become acquainted with the theoretical foundations of music, and this was probably also Gade's motivation for delegating part of his theory teaching.

8   William Behrend (ed.), *Minder om Niels W. Gade. Kendte Mænds og Kvinders Erindringer* [Remembrances of Gade. Reminiscences of famous men and women], Copenhagen 1930, 83-84.
9   Organist Johannes Beck, in Behrend, *op. cit.*, 59-60.

The newspaper *København* maintained that the actual reason why Rosenhoff at the end of the academic year 1891 sought to formalise his right to guide his students to their finals was that Otto Malling had guided some of Rosenhoff's students to the examination:

> Malling, who inherited Gade's chair, held an examination in composition shortly before Christmas. He had compositions performed by two ladies who for three years had been students of Rosenhoff and only in the last of these three years had been taught by Malling. This 'skimming off the cream' of Rosenhoff's work had the effect that the latter made moves to have his position changed for the better ...[10]

In the same issue of the newspaper there was also a reply from Malling, who declared that he had naturally wanted to show the results of his tuition: 'That is why I presented the written work they [the students] had produced and why I had them play the miniatures they had composed. That there were, by coincidence, a couple of Rosenhoff's students among them was not something I could really do anything about.'[11]

To the journalist's enquiry whether the students in question had not been trained in 'composition' by Rosenhoff, Malling answered:

> Possibly he had given them a simple task once in a while. But the subject he actually took them for was harmony and counterpoint – in other words just theory. I cannot believe that Gade handed over to him more authority. In any case the registers indicate that Gade kept *all* his students in his classes right to the end.[12]

Malling agreed, however, that the Conservatory produced 'too many inferior female teachers, and that the exams should be arranged more sensibly – but that is the kind of thing one is unwilling to talk too much about'.

Apart from adopting a non-conflictual position with regard to criticisms of the Conservatory, Malling therefore also played down the theoretical subjects – harmony and counterpoint – that Rosenhoff placed so much emphasis on. And what-

---

10 *København* 26.2.1892. Article signed *Presto*. The two young ladies were Christiane Rützow-Olsen (1870-1962) and Tekla Griebel Wandall (1865-1940), as appears from Rosenhoff's application to the Board of Directors, enclosed in the file at the Ministry of Culture (see note 4, above).
11 *København* 26.2.1892. Article signed *Kurt*.
12 *Ibid.*

ever a pair of female pupils of Rosenhoff had managed to compose on the basis of the latter's elementary instruction could consequently not be characterised as other than 'miniatures'.

The Board of Directors of the Conservatory had for many years consisted of the triumvirate of Hartmann, Gade and Paulli, but after Gade's death in December 1890 and Paulli's resignation in April 1891 it came to consist of Hartmann, August Winding, Carl Helsted and Friedrich Julius Georg Vilhelm Stemann. The expansion with a fourth member – Stemann, who was Head of Department in the Ministry of Culture – was motivated by the fact that since 1883-84 the Conservatory had been in receipt of an economic subsidy from the State,[13] which made for a legitimate public interest in the affairs of the institution.

When Rosenhoff received the unexpected decision that the Board of the Conservatory had rejected his application, he first thought that it was 'Professor Helsted and Head of Department Stemann' who must have had most say in it, and when he asked August Winding why the Board had changed its opinion, Winding answered that 'his father-in-law [Hartmann] did not recall having had a conversation' with Rosenhoff about the matter. As the reason for his own changed attitude Winding gave 'the vague and evasive answer: "We did not believe that you were serious in wanting to leave us" etc. etc.' Rosenhoff concluded, 'I then understood that I had been sacrificed for the sake of other interests, and I bade Hr. Winding and the Conservatory farewell.'[14]

Rosenhoff therefore found that the Board was split into two factions, with Hartmann and his son-in-law Winding making up the weaker one, Helsted and Stemann the powerful one. In pointing to the last two as responsible for having turned down his application, Rosenhoff was at the same time indicating that it was Hartmann and Winding who were advocates for everything remaining as it was, while Helsted and Stemann stood for an attitude of greater renewal.

Rosenhoff himself had set the stage for a peaceful co-existence with his colleagues by establishing the boundaries between the subjects:

> But it soon became clear that such a discussion about the students' needs was not to be allowed. Right at the beginning of the new academic year I sought to initiate one such discussion with Professor Malling, but I was turned away with the remark that our subjects did not have anything to do with one another. Later in the year, when it became apparent that a discussion could nonetheless not be entirely avoided, he defined his view of the demarcation between our subjects in terms of its being my job *to teach the students what they*

---

13 Hammerich, *op. cit.*, 40.
14 *Dagens Nyheder* 25.2.1892. Article by Orla Rosenhoff, entitled 'The Conservatory of Music'.

could all learn, whereas it fell solely to him to make it possible for the students (especially the talented ones) to make practical use of their theoretical knowledge – as already stated, a completely impossible task with respect to the entire student body of the Conservatory – and I then felt that my position in reality was reduced to that of *teaching assistant*.[15] [Rosenhoff's emphasis]

Rosenhoff's arguments made no impression on the Board, however, which merely brushed him aside with the comment that it did not see itself as being in a position to interfere 'by *fiat*... in an arrangement that was deliberately established by the Board of Directors itself a year ago, and to take students from Professor Malling against his wishes, once they have been entrusted to him.'[16]

With this the Board therefore assented to an arrangement that consisted in 'Music theory's third discipline (form in conjunction with instrumentation and music history)' only being offered to a portion of the students, just as it approved that only Malling should handle this part of the curriculum. If we ignore instrumentation,[17] which must be seen as a highly specialised discipline for the benefit especially of composers in the making, it was therefore subjects such as form and music history that were thereby isolated from practical music education, i.e. subjects which could have instilled in the students some analytical tools for comprehending the formal construction of musical works, and could also have helped them to reflect on the historical and aesthetic dimensions in music.

The evening edition of *Berlingske Tidende* of 25 February 1892 printed a statement from the Conservatory's oldest director, Hartmann, who did not directly deny that he had at first been sympathetically inclined to Rosenhoff's suggestion:

... if, as has been said, in certain quarters in the meantime or beforehand some sympathy for, or at any rate understanding of, Hr. Rosenhoff's wishes may have been unofficially voiced (viewed exclusively from his particular point of view), it is nevertheless clear that such remarks could only have been made under the firm condition that agreement on the matter be reached between the two teachers.

Thus Hartmann did not wish to deny that Rosenhoff's demands were reasonable, but he maintained that the support of the Board would have been conditional on Malling and Rosenhoff reaching agreement on the allocation of students. To this we should

---

15 *Dagens Nyheder* 25.2.1892.
16 *København* 26.2.1892.
17 Malling published *Instrumentationslære til Brug ved Undervisning og til Selvstudium* [A Manual of Instrumentation for Teaching and Self-tuition], Copenhagen 1894.

merely add that if such agreement had been reached, then Rosenhoff's approach to the Board would have surely been superfluous, and in such a case Hartmann would not have been called upon to take a position on the problem!

But the consequence of the Board's lack of backing was that Rosenhoff's threat to leave the Conservatory came into force. Whether he 'went' or 'was pushed' is in this connection not nearly as interesting as to seek out the reason why the conflict between him and Malling had such a drastic outcome.

The coverage of the affair in the press shows that there was broad dissatisfaction with the Conservatory's attitude: a dissatisfaction, which especially focused on unapproachability and nepotism, but to a certain extent also on professional standards and aims. For example, *København* reported:

> In general it is high time that conditions at the Conservatory should be publicly examined. Over 25 years the public has been systematically kept out of its business. Its examinations have been held in conditions of strictest secrecy, so that no uninitiated person could gain admission to the mysteries of the inner sanctum, nor have even managed to sneak in. This secretiveness – which conceals a fair amount of tyranny exerted by the family that seems to have monopolized all teaching positions for its own and its friends' use – must soon come to an end. With its 10,000 kroner of government subsidy, the Conservatory of Music can no longer behave like a private institution. We must see it in the full daylight of public scrutiny.
>
> The Rosenhoff affair will perhaps contribute a little towards cleaning up the Conservatory's conditions. We did not gain much respect for its activities through reading Hr. Hammerich's pointless *Festschrift* and Hr. Bondesen's pretentious statistics about the numerous, nameless female music teachers ... the Conservatory has churned out.[18]

The accusation of nepotism was of course directed at the omnipresent Hartmann-Gade dynasty, which for good or ill had controlled the Conservatory throughout its 25-year existence, either through members of that dynasty occupying the teaching positions or by itself neglecting the need to discuss the institutions aims. Even the otherwise loyal Angul Hammerich, who was only distantly related to the Hartmann family,[19] does not disguise in the Conservatory's silver jubilee report that there were originally more extensive plans for the institution than those that had been come to

18 *København* 17.2.1892.
19 Hammerich's mother, Julie Scheuermann, was a cousin of Hartmann's first wife, Emma Zinn, and had grown up with her in the Zinns' merchants' house at 3 Kvæsthusgade by Copenhagen harbour.

pass; for example, with respect to offering orchestral playing and as regards music history: 'the lectures that were in prospect for various musical subjects – music history, aesthetics and the like – did not work well to any significant extent. In connection with classes in form, Gade later took it upon himself to impart occasional music-historical information.'[20]

'Occasional music-historical information', which moreover was only offered to the most talented students, was therefore all that the original fine intentions had produced.

We may suppose that the appointment of Helsted and Stemann to the Board of Directors of the Conservatory was motivated precisely by the wish to clean up the Conservatory's operations, and that this project was presumably reckoned to have the best chance of success after Gade's death. The appointment of Otto Malling to Gade's former position, which is to say maintaining Gade's powers, was presumably an element in such a 'cleaning plan', whereas there was scarcely a thought of removing Rosenhoff from his post. That the conflict nevertheless had this result can be blamed on the fact that he was the sacrifice in an undeclared power-struggle between the two factions on the Board, of which the now weak but previously powerful one had not previously had a need to argue for its arrangements and therefore did not actively back up Rosenhoff's request (cf. August Winding's reply: 'We did not believe that you were serious' and Hartmann's evasive observation that the Board's support was conditional on the two teachers reaching agreement), while the two strong members of the Board – Helsted and Stemann – either did not understand the significance of holding on to such a committed and progressive teacher, or perhaps did not dare to restrict Malling's freedom of action. Rosenhoff's dismissal was therefore hardly a consequence of anyone wanting to be rid of him, but rather of the *precautions* that had been taken in order to counter, amongst other things, nepotism and lack of transparency at the Conservatory.

If it was the intention to stamp out nepotism, one must recognise that this did not succeed either. For in place of Rosenhoff the director's son, Gustav Helsted, was appointed. This 'matter of personnel' was also discussed in the press, where it was reported that the appointment had happened without Stemann's knowledge, and that when he discovered what had happened, Stemann demanded that the post should be advertised.[21] The practice of filling teaching positions with family members had thus in reality simply passed from one family to another! In 1895 Rosenhoff was given a State pension,[22] presumably with Stemann's collaboration, which can probably be understood as a sticking-plaster on the wound.

---

20 Hammerich, *op. cit.*, 23.
21 *København* 17.2.1892.
22 Sophus Albert Emil Hagen, 'Rosenhoff, Orla Albert Vilhelm', in *Carl Frederik Bricka* (ed.), *Dansk biografisk Lexicon*, [Danish Biographical Lexicon], Copenhagen 1900, vol. 14.

A protest concert

For obvious reasons it cannot be determined whether it would have contributed to theoretical subjects gaining a more central position in music education had Rosenhoff remained at the Conservatory. But his insistence on the placing of music theory and music history in the broader picture was precisely one of Rosenhoff's most distinctive characteristics as a teacher, and this is borne out by, amongst others, his private pupil Hilda Sehested. In 1888 she was in Bayreuth, where she heard a Wagner opera for the first time, which made a deep impression on her:

> Here it's not a question of an aesthetic entertainment, lightly presented and received. Something much more serious is happening. ... Incidentally I very much long for once to have the opportunity to talk with a very clever man, preferably Rosenhoff, about these things; there are issues that are too big for me, which I cannot deal with, and which make my head ache. It's especially the relationship of 'abstract' music to the dramatic. The significance of Wagner and Brahms in relation to one another – this division of music into two mighty branches during the developments of the past 20 years – that's the kind of questions (and in a way I think they concern the historical side of things) that I cannot deal with, and which I long for the clever person I just named to explain to me.[23]

Apparently, it was burning aesthetic questions of this kind that Rosenhoff was prepared to discuss with his students: the division of music into a New German tendency represented by Wagner and Liszt and a classicistic tendency represented by Brahms. Nielsen too stressed that it was one of Rosenhoff's valuable qualities that he was willing to discuss the latest musical developments with his students: 'His knowledge as well as his taste are on the same level, and as a teacher he is invaluable, because at the same time as insisting on strictness in harmony and counterpoint, he nonetheless pays tribute to modern outlooks of the freest kinds.'[24]

Anger over Rosenhoff's dismissal was so great that a group of his pupils felt called up to react. On 1 April 1892 they held a benefit concert in the lesser hall of the Concert Palæ for an invited audience, and in order not to be short of public attention for the aims of their concert they also invited the press. *Politiken*'s reviewer Charles Kjerulf began by mentioning that the concert was intended as a protest against the leadership of the Conservatory:

---

23 Letter from Hilda Sehested to Inger Marie Bockelund, 20.9.1888. Inger Marie Bockelund's private archive. Rigsarkivet. Cited in Tine Bagger Sørensen and Dorrit Vejen Hansen, *Hilda Sehested (1858-1936). En dansk komponists liv og musik* [Life and Work of a Danish Composer]. Major dissertation, University of Copenhagen, Musicological Institute, April 1993.

24 John Fellow (ed.), *Carl Nielsen til sin samtid*, Copenhagen 1999, 50.

The actual occasion for the concert, Hr. Rosenhoff's disgraceful removal from Copenhagen's Conservatory of Music, has been publicly debated in the papers, both by himself and by the leadership of the Conservatory, so that there is little or no point in making any secret of the pupils' protest concert.[25]

Berlingske Tidende stressed that according to the invitation the concert was being held by 'two ladies and four gentlemen "who have all studied the theory of composition' (or better, just 'theory of composition') under Orla Rosenhoff.'[26] After 'the rather long concert of student works', the review concluded by clarifying: 'Of the six composers, only Mr. Carl Nielsen enjoyed Mr. Rosenhoff's instruction at the Conservatory of Music; the other five are private pupils.' So it was important for the newspaper to underline that the loss of Rosenhoff was nothing to speak of from the Conservatory's point of view, since only one of the composers – even the most talented – had received instruction from Rosenhoff as a pupil at the Conservatory; the others had been private pupils and had not made a particularly interesting impression. *Nationaltidende*'s reviewer seems to have chimed in with *Berlingske Tidende*, for in this newspaper too it was emphasized that of the six it was only Nielsen who had studied with Rosenhoff at the Conservatory. Both papers were therefore inclined to play down the significance of Rosenhoff's dismissal.[27]

The protest concert consisted of music by Hother Ploug (Theme and Variations for two Violins, Viola and Cello), Rudolph Berg (Waltz for piano duet), Hilda Sehested (four little Fantasy Pieces), George Dupont-Hansen (Four Little Piano Pieces, Op. 1), Emma Verdier (Five Songs) and last but not not least Nielsen – his String Quintet, which had been premiered three years earlier. That the concert made a rather protracted impression and presented music by composers who did not go on to make a name for themselves in Danish musical life does not alter the fact that a handful of young, indignant composers hereby demonstrated solidarity with a man whom they considered to be the blameless victim of an obscure power game. Internally it may also have contributed to strengthening the solidarity between them and to confirming their conviction that the musical world was divided into *them* and *us*.

It is very likely that the young Rosenhoff pupils had already several years earlier formed a performing circle; thus Nielsen in 1887 informed his girlfriend Emilie Demant that Rosenhoff considered his newly composed string quartet to be so successful that he wanted to propose its performance in a little music society that he intended to form. In his letter he quoted Rosenhoff as saying 'for I am in the process of forming a society, which will be called The Society of Composers (Componistforening). All our

25 *Politiken* 5.4.1892.
26 *Berlingske Tidende* (evening edition) 2.4.1892.
27 *Nationaltidende* (evening edition) 2.4.1892.

finest musicians and a number of aristocratic families support my initiative, and so I think that your quartet should have its first performance there.'[28]

In a letter of December 1887 to Hilda Sehested, Rosenhoff also discussed his idea to found a private musical society that was to be called 'Floridus'.[29] The article on Rosenhoff in the first edition of the *Danish Biographical Lexicon* states that such a society was founded by his pupils 'in recognition of his importance as a music pedagogue', and that 'on his departure from the Conservatory of Music it honoured him in various ways.'[30] Although there is not much information about the 'Floridus' society, it is known that on at least one occasion in 1895 it held a public concert at the Concert Palæ.[31] These facts indicate that it existed for a number of years and may have begun to be active as early as 1888, which is to say long before Rosenhoff ran into difficulties at the Conservatory. In other words he considered it important that his pupils should have a chance to have their compositions tried out in practice, and he strove to establish a framework for such musical try-outs. But despite the fact that he supported his students so actively, there was still no question that he wanted to promote them at any price. For example, in 1894 Nielsen sought to persuade Rosenhoff to write an article about him for a German paper, which could then be cited in a Danish paper, which Rosenhoff refused to do:

> But that [Wilhelm] Behrend and I should write an article at your behest for a German paper, so that the same article should later appear in Danish papers as a *true* indication of what is being said in Germany about the composer Carl Nielsen – no, my dear friend, isn't that a bit steep? ... spare me, please .. the right person will surely appear out there – just give it time!!![32]

Nielsen and Rosenhoff did not fall out over the episode; on the contrary Nielsen later counted Rosenhoff as his most important teacher (see the introduction to this article), and at Rosenhoff's funeral in 1905 he gave a fine speech, in which he sought to put his finger on some of his teacher's qualities:

---

28 Letter from Nielsen to Emilie Demant 24.12.1887, reproduced in John Fellow (ed.), *Carl Nielsen Brevudgaven* vol. 1, Copenhagen 2005, 57.

29 Orla Rosenhoff to Hilda Sehested, 21.12.1887. Hilda Sehested, private archive no. 6344, A12. Rigsarkivet. The letter also includes a draft programme for the first concert, which was to consist of an introductory cantata, Hilda Sehested's String Quartet in F, songs with piano by Hother Ploug, and songs for female voices and piano by Thyra Schiøler. It is not known whether a concert with this programme took place.

30 Hagen, *op. cit.*.

31 The concert was reviewed in *Dannebrog* 19.4.1895 and included music by Emil Krag-Juel-Vind-Frijs, Thyra Schiøler and Hilda Sehested.

32 Letter from Orla Rosenhoff to Nielsen, 30.10.1894, reproduced in John Fellow (ed.), *Carl Nielsen Brevudgaven* vol. 1, Copenhagen 2005, 368-369.

We, his pupils, will always remember Orla Rosenhoff; in a way he has made it impossible for us not to, because in future we will not be able to engage in teaching, influencing or guiding the younger generation without thinking about him – the fine, true teacher and educator, both strict in his demands and at the same time kind and understanding in his judgments when he saw someone making a good effort, or just an effort in the right direction – and probably all of us can truly say that we are grateful to have known him.[33]

As an introduction to his pedagogic methods, Rosenhoff published several collections of instructional material, including *450 firstemmige Opgaver som Materiale til Brug ved den musiktheoretiske Undervisning* (450 Four-part Exercises for Use in Music-theory Classes),[34] to which his pupil Carl Cohn in 1909 added a *Nøgle til Løsning af Orla Rosenhoffs firstemmige Opgaver* (Key to the Solution of Orla Rosenhoff's Four-part Exercises).[35] Cohn's *Key* was warmly reviewed by Nielsen, who once again used the opportunity to hail Rosenhoff for his system of tuition and for the unselfish attitude he brought to his role as educator:

He approached this task with an unusual and comprehensive cultural awareness, sharp intelligence, and the brilliance and character that are the fruits of resignation from the field of production. Through a series of noble and finely crafted compositions he had reached the conclusion that it was not as a composer that he could really excel. Therefore he threw himself passionately into music theory, and here he managed to give us the best we have in that area.[36]

The saying 'To whomsoever God gives a task, to him He also gives the understanding of it' can be interpreted such that whoever is given a job is at the same time given

---

33 John Fellow (ed.), *Carl Nielsen til sin samtid*, 1999, 54.

34 *450 firstemmige Opgaver som Materiale til Brug ved den musiktheoretiske Undervisning*. Copenhagen, n.d., first collection, vol. 1, first collection vol. 2.

35 *Nøgle til Løsning af Orla Rosenhoffs firstemmige Opgaver til Brug ved Undervisningen i Harmonielære*, Copenhagen and Leipzig, 1909. Carl Cohn (1874-1939) who had lost his eyesight as a child, had private tuition in piano and music theory from Victor Bendix and Orla Rosenhoff and appeared on many occasions as a concert pianist. He worked for many years as a music teacher at the Institute for the Blind and was also the first national president for the Danish Society for the Blind. In 1914 he took his wife's surname and called himself Carl Cohn Haste.

36 John Fellow (ed.), *Carl Nielsen til sin samtid*, 1999, 140. Nielsen's review, printed in *Vort Land* 21.10.1909, emphasized amongst other things the importance of being able to modulate exclusively by means of pure triads, i.e. without altered chords and chromaticism, which prompted commentaries from Asger Juul and Carl Cohn that Nielsen in turn answered in *Vort Land* 2.11.1909.

some influence on how that job should be managed. Orla Rosenhoff set a definitive stamp on theory instruction at the Conservatory, but staked his position – and lost – when he was refused permission to guide his pupils all the way to the final examination. Otto Malling, who did not share (literally) Rosenhoff's interest in offering an optimal education in music theory to all, but devoted himself to tuition in instrumentation to a select few, covered himself with glory as an efficient administrator. It fell to Malling to mark out the course for the Conservatory's educational politics at the beginning of the 20th century.

Translated by David Fanning

ABSTRACT

The article takes as its starting point press coverage of the dismissal in 1892 of Orla Rosenhoff, teacher of music theory at the Royal Danish Conservatory of Music. The aim is to throw light on the position of theoretical subjects in the curriculum during Nielsen's years as a student, and also to discuss the status of the Conservatory at that time. It appears that after Gade's death a number of antagonistic attitudes to the significance of music theory for practical performance came to the surface. Rosenhoff, who was an important source of support and inspiration for Nielsen, argued that all students should be offered tuition in music theory on a certain level; his view did not prevail, however, and later on music theory and history were to be downgraded in the context of practical musical education.

MUSIC AND PHILOSOPHY

By Finn Mathiassen

Danish society, which for good or ill provided the foundation for Carl Nielsen's existence as man and artist, was, like any other society in what was then called 'the civilised world', a social formation on the way towards bourgeois democracy, industriali-
sation and the total dominance of the capitalist system of production. This development pursued its own particular paths in Denmark; of relevance here was the fact
that our social economy, and the country's well-being as a whole, was dependent on
agriculture in a different way from any other nation. But the main tendency was the
same as everywhere else. There was no agreement as to where that tendency was
leading or what lay behind it, but it was as clear as day that the world was not what it
had been. And more and more people were coming to think that it was not what it
should be either. For artists the situation in Nielsen's time had long since become
precarious. Externally a kind of privatisation had taken place: only vestiges remained
of the once so solid material and ideological links between art and feudal society, and
between art and the autocracy of the authorities and institutions created by God.
Now each and every artistic initiative was obliged to assert itself in the conditions of
a free market. Internally the situation can be briefly and very broadly summed up in
one word: alienation. Art, which in some Golden Age or other – perhaps even in one
as close at hand as the artist's own childhood milieu – had been in general like an elementary necessity of life, was now forced to justify itself as saleable and profitable, as
a luxury or a secular status-symbol, an object for snobbery and secular worship, and all
this within the framework of the self-created institution of bourgeois cultural life,
which for many a sincerely striving artist came to represent a Vanity Fair. Art was certainly in demand, but not respected, and as for 'an elementary necessity of life', this
was hardly the case for anyone other than the artist himself. He (and the few women
who had the chance to make their mark) was potentially left out in the cold and risked
perceiving himself at any moment – as befell Carl Nielsen – as a 'foolish fantast'.

Individual artists naturally reacted to this situation according to their own individual preoccupations, and with very varied results. But here again we can perceive
a general tendency: artists were forced to reflect – they had inherited what Thorkil

Kjems has labelled an 'ideological problematics of production'.[1] To be a composer, for example, had since Beethoven implied a latent requirement for reflection on the ways of the world, on the meaning of life and on music's place within it all; the eternal question 'What is Music?', which until then had in essence figured as an academic problem in the philosophy of philosophers, had become the burning question for a composer's philosophy. It appeared in all sorts of forms, from public polemics and solemn manifestos to serious articles, but the general aim was for composers, as for artists as a whole, to justify art's *subjective* necessity of life – which they themselves felt in their bones — as a social, cosmic or divine, but at any rate supra-personal, *objective* necessity of life.

Like so many authentic artists of the time – as distinct from mere purveyors of art – Nielsen also gave some attention to philosophical matters. Admittedly he may have asked himself whether 'at the end of the day those people are right who say "just don't think". Shouldn't sunshine and blue sky be our only concern?',[2] and indeed neither Palestrina, Bach, Mozart nor any other of his great models had left behind utterances that pointed to any great philosophical interest. Nevertheless he felt compelled. To the very last he grappled with the question of the 'reason for everything' – 'Why do I compose and you sculpt?' he wrote at the age of 61 to his wife.[3] His diaries and letters, newspaper and periodical contributions, reviews and interviews, and *My Childhood*, are brimming over with genuine philosophising; orally too he left behind many a pearl of wisdom. In the course of time he reached more definitive statements in the form of a series of essays, feature articles and the like, which he gathered together and published in 1925 under the title *Living Music*. That same year he wrote his 'Meditations',[4] which are not only a valuable example of his lively and colourful prose, but also contain in concentrated form some of his most important views. He did not bequeath any kind of philosophical *summa*; that was not his object in life. He never went further than sporadic contributions, but from these we can glimpse a philosophy that was not only consistent but also authentic: a philosophy behind which stood his entire personality.

---

1 Thorkil Kjems, 'Tristans problematik' [The problematics of *Tristan*] (Master's thesis, Musicological Institute, University of Århus, 1984). The dissertation is a pilot project for a deeper investigation into the effect of ideology problematics in music.

2 *Mon ikke til syvende og sidst de Mennesker har Ret, som siger: bare ikke tænke. Mon ikke Solens Lys og den blaa Luft burde være al vor Stræben?* Letter from Nielsen to Bror Beckman (begun 29 October 1910, continued 6 November), John Fellow (ed.), *Carl Nielsen Brevudgaven*, vol. 3, Copenhagen 2007, 556.

3 *Grunden til alting... . Hvorfor skriver jeg Musik og Du former?* Letter of 19 March 1927, Torben Schousboe (ed.), *Carl Nielsen: Dagbøger og brevveksling med Anne Marie Carl-Nielsen*, Copenhagen 1983, 520.

4 See John Fellow (ed.), *Carl Nielsen til sin samtid*, Copenhagen 1999, 328-340.

Nielsen was not an especially well-read person. His schooling had not gone beyond the thatched village school, and throughout his life he was eager to broaden his spiritual horizons, not least through keen reading of philosophical literature. But he was not omnivorous. His favourite author was Plato (he was especially taken by *The Republic*), and on the whole the ancient philosophers seem to have been part of his core reading. On the other hand he was ignorant of the greater part of more recent philosophy, from Kant onwards, and it is especially noticeable that neither Schopenhauer nor Nietzsche, who played such a prominent role for many of his contemporaries (such as Gustav Mahler, Richard Strauss and others), gets so much as a mention, any more than do the writings of Richard Wagner or Eduard Hanslick. That he was acquainted with them, if not from his own reading then through conversations and discussions with friends and artistic colleagues, is surely beyond doubt; these writings were part of the compulsory homework for his intellectual contemporaries. But his reactions were hardly positive.[5] In his philosophical concerns, just as in his music, he felt that he had to look behind these people, all the way home to the Classics. What he found there he took on board not as ready-made answers, but as an incitement and guide to his own continued searchings. And that was what he needed. Despite all his reading and other intellectual impulses, his philosophy was no mere academic school trip, but a personal wrestling with a task that was no more possible for him to avoid than it was for other artists of the time: namely to substantiate the subjective life-necessity of art as an objective one.

He engaged with the matter in his own way. Not for him the whole intellectual *fin-de-siècle* ideology, with its pessimism, mysticism, nostalgia, cultivation of *l'art pour l'art* and esoteric sects. He had come in fresh from the Danish countryside, where no one knew about anything of that sort, and when he encountered the problems, as he inevitably had to, he tackled them from the bottom up.

---

5 Whatever ideas Nielsen may have adopted from Schopenhauer (via Wagner?) and Nietzsche he in any case turned upside down. When the Preface to the Fourth Symphony asserts that music '*is* life, whereas the other [arts] only represent and paraphrase life', that corresponds closely to Schopenhauer's view of music as the immediate expression of the *Wille zum Leben* that constitutes *The World*. And Nielsen's continuation — that 'life is inexhaustible and inextinguishable: a continuing succession of conflict, struggle, procreation and death, and everything returns [in a cycle]' – that may be (and probably is, even if it its hard to understand how he would know it) an echo of Nietzsche's *Zarathustra*-idea about *die ewige Wiederkunft*. But while Life, the Will and the World for Schopenhauer stood as intolerable evils, and the idea of eternal return for Nietzsche represented a superhuman challenge, Nielsen's sympathies were entirely on the side of Life, Will and the World, and the idea that 'everything returns' is celebrated in the Fourth Symphony as an unequivocal triumph for everything and everyone that has a share in life.

'Music is life...'

That art was a basic necessity of life for Nielsen is one of the most certain things that can be said about him. To compose music was the only real possibility he had to fully confirm his right to life, and he suffered in those periods of latency or recharging that preceded many of his larger projects; he never knew whether it would work at all, and each time he felt as though he had to begin again from scratch. On the other hand, once he had finally 'switched on' (his own expression) he seldom knew how it would turn out. Instead he raced along, and the motor — a highly personal combination of instinct and reflection, musical-visionary fantasy and technical know-how, all united in intense concentration – was as a rule sufficiently robust not to stall at obstacles encountered along the way. When his concentration was at its height and his psyche engaged from top to bottom, he came to experience what it truly means to 'be absorbed' in a piece of work:

> Then it's as though my personal will is absent or so attenuated that the project itself takes hold of me, to the extent that I — that is the person I am — am dissolved and as though cast to the winds and floating in space. I have told you that when I was working on *Maskarade* I sometimes had the impression of being like a large drainpipe, through which there flowed a stream I could do absolutely nothing about.[6]

This was the positive joy of work that Nielsen experienced, but in the strongly intensified form that since time immemorial has been the driving force behind all genuine art. Many of his contemporary artists experienced this power as something supernatural, as a mystical revelation of the true connection of things beyond all earthly dualisms, and thereby as the objective justification for their artistic striving. This revelation became the personal-empirical point of departure for many an artist-philosopher and the basis for many an ideology of art at the time, not least for symbolism, which in Denmark gained a footing thanks to those behind the 'spiritual breakthrough' of the 1890s, with its profound impact on a significant part of Danish literature and painting in the period leading up to the First World War.

For Nielsen too, the ecstasy of artistic work became of fundamental importance for his thinking about the world, life and music. His ideas could soar high

---

6 *Saa er det nemlig som om min personlige Villie er borte eller saa slappet at det er Sagen der tager mig i den Grad at jeg x: det Menneske jeg er – er opløst og ligesom udkastet i Luften og svævende i alting. Jeg har fortalt Dig, at da jeg arbejdede på "Maskarade" havde jeg af og til den Forestilling at jeg var som et stort Drænrør hvorigennem der løb en Strøm, jeg aldeles ikke kunde gøre for.* Letter from Nielsen to his wife, 10 July 1914; Schousboe, *op. cit.*, 387.

and wide, but he always only breathed the air of our own planet. He kept both feet on the ground, and in that respect if he has to be classified at all it has to be with those behind 'the breakthrough of the common people', the Jutland poets, the first worker-authors and the Funen 'farmer-painters '.[7] His level-headedness can still today have an almost coarse effect, and for many in his own day it must often have appeared as pure sacrilege. For example, he kept a clear, sceptical distance from such a hallowed term as 'inspiration', with all it subsumes. 'Stop waiting for moods', he wrote to his Swedish colleague Wilhelm Stenhammar, who had come to a halt with a piece of work:

> Try and start off with long semibreves, like dry cantus firmi, like wooden beams that are laid out to provide the base of the house, like boring, rough cornerstones on which to build. You are a master of counterpoint, so use it.[8]

Secular handiwork enthroned; maybe so, but not as the be-all and end-all of art, only as a dignified and modest entry-point to *artistic* work.

What Nielsen experienced, while the artistic process lasted, was that his ego and his will, thoughts and feelings gave way in obedience towards something that he strove all through his life to give a name. His most successful attempt to name it is set out in a comparison with which he introduced a 1922 newspaper review of some newly published Danish songs by Thomas Laub:

7   Nielsen's life coincided with a period in Danish history whose striking dynamic in all areas of society his contemporaries were already seeking to define by talking about various kinds of 'breakthrough' – in this case 'of the soul' and 'of the common people ' — roughly as in our time there has been talk of 'trends'. For Nielsen this kind of thing held no interest whatsoever. He loved and admired Jeppe Aakjær's poems 'beyond thinking, beyond reservations, but as a rich gift from the beloved son of the Danish soil' (*uden Tanke, uden Kritik, men som en rig Gave fra den danske Jords elskede Søn*; letter to Theodor Wellejus, 20.4.1928, in Eggert Møller and Torben Meyer (eds.), *Carl Nielsens Breve*, 254) and he was delighted to have Fritz Syberg's painting of a Funen courtyard hanging in his study (see Anne Marie Telmányi, *Anne Marie Carl-Nielsen*, Copenhagen 1979, 85). He was and remained a son of the soil, specifically of the Danish soil. But to be loved was something that was hard to obtain, and when it was a question of really important matters — in his constant craving to experience the redeeming power of art, and in his frictions with an uncomprehending, disorientated age — there he had kindred spirits in two artists who are generally reckoned among the symbolists, namely J.F. Willumsen and Sophus Claussen, both of them friends from his youth. Their mutual relations, both personal and artistic, deserve closer investigation.
8   *Lad være med at vente paa Stemninger. Tag og begynd med lange, halve Noder, som tørre Cantus firmi, som Træbjælker der skal ligge og danne Grundformen for Huset, som kedelige grove Hjørnesten, hvor man gaar ud fra. Du er jo en Mester i Kontrapunkt, benyt det.* Letter of 17.9.1921, in Eggert Møller and Torben Meyer (eds.), *Carl Nielsens Breve*, 209.

Anyone who has walked the St. Gotthard pass in spring must surely have noticed the water in the little lake of melted snow at the top. It stands and vibrates, as though it cannot make up its mind. And yet it has to make a choice. The four rivers that spring from this place suck water in different directions , so that there is no point in resisting.

And should *we* just stand and rot?

And what about free will?

Let's not go into this, but simply rejoice at Nature's great, clear writing, which brings us to a halt and makes us reflect on the universal laws of life, both those that concern matter and those that we observe in what we call our spiritual life. They are one and the same ... [9]

'The universal laws of life': by this expression Nielsen understood nothing supernatural, magical or mystical. The philosophy that underpinned it is worldly through and through, and his comparison is actually not a comparison at all. The forces that made the indecisive water flow where it was supposed to and had to, were naturally not the same as the powers that directed Nielsen to the right outlet for *his* abundance. Matter and spirit are not identical. But they are two sides of one and the same thing: Nature. And they are both thereby subject to the same codex: the laws of all life. 'Music is life...' he wrote in the Preface to his Fourth Symphony. That should be understood literally. It was a definition; and what did he mean by 'life'?

For Nielsen the term Life was bound up with the notion of things that moved, that came into being, existed, and ceased, from inner necessity and by virtue of their own being: by their nature in other words, and thereby – and this for him was no mere play on words – were in harmony with Nature. With the passing years the term came to mean more and more for him, until eventually it embraced the entire cosmic reality from atoms and microbes to the paths of the planets across the firmament, with man and the animals on the green earth somewhere in the middle – in short it embraced everything that no one can speculate or fantasize about, but everything that is possible for any healthy and observant person to absorb through his senses

---

9   *Enhver, der har vandret over St. Gotthard i Foraarstiden, har sikkert lagt Mærke til Vandet i den lille Sø af smeltet Sne, som findes på Toppen. Det staar og dirrer, som om det ikke kan beslutte sig. Og dog må der træffes et Valg. De fire Strømme, der har deres Udspring fra dette Sted, suger hver sin Vej, saa det nytter ikke at stritte imod. – Vi vil da heller ikke staa her og raadne!*

    Og den fri vilje?

    Lad os ikke komme ind herpaa, men glæde os over Naturens store, tydelige Skrift, der standser os og bringer os til Eftertanke om Lovene for alt Liv, saavel dem, der gælder Materien som dem, vi ser i det, vi kalder det aandelige Liv. De er de selv samme [...] . *Levende Musik* ("Danske Sange"), Copenhagen 1925, 61; *Living Music*, London n.d., 50; John Fellow (1999) *op. cit.* ("Nye Sange"), 248.

and to process by means of his understanding and fantasy. For Nielsen, forces opposed to *life* were therefore naturally *death* – the absence of all movement – , but in a characteristic coupling with notions of non-Nature: affectation, sentimentality, conditioning, robotic discipline, in general everything forced, rootless and unnatural.

So much for Nielsen's understanding of the word Life. But what did he mean by speaking of its Laws? Words like 'law', 'law-abiding' and others with the same content belong to the weightiest he deployed with his pen. By them he understood nothing of the order of juridical paragraphs or moral precepts; nor did his concept of Laws correspond to that of the natural sciences , or mathematics or logic. And it is an important fact that it had nothing to do with any form of normative aesthetics either, for example with rules of musical composition. When he talked enthusiastically at one point of 'legitimate counterpoint',[10] this was – with all due respect to good craftsmanship – not with Bellermann's or anyone else's textbook in mind. Nor did the musical Laws have anything to do with 'mechanical polyphony', which he found so repulsive in Wagner's *Meistersinger* Prelude. Rather they had to do with an 'organic polyphony',[11] one of the many forms of a fantasy-borne manifestation of Music's own being, and precisely for that reason allied to Nature and its 'laws for all life'. And to pin down that kind of law in words, never mind in paragraphs, prescriptions or rules, could not be done. Nielsen's 'laws for all life' were, properly understood, incomprehensible, raised above all theorising as much as they were above any day-to-day conception of transgression and punishment, cause and effect – but all the same very real: the only laws that were able unswervingly to uphold themselves in his presence.

To 'hear with the eyes, see with the ears, smell with the hands, think with the heart, and feel with the brain'

Much has been said and written about Nielsen's 'originality', pointing especially to his peculiarly direct relationship to musical material, as though he had only just fallen in love, cf. his famous words, cited in and out of season, about the third as 'a gift of God, a fourth as an experience and a fifth as the highest joy'.[12] And with justice. But when — as has happened so often, and not without consequences in Danish musical life — people have wanted to connect this originality with notions of his music's 'absolute' character and its 'purity', that has been a fruitless chase. Admittedly

---

10 The expression came from Max Brod. See Karl Clausen: 'Max Brod og Carl Nielsen', in *Oplevelser og studier omkring Carl Nielsen* [Carl Nielsen: Experiences and Studies], Tønder 1966, pp. 13ff.

11 'Mozart og vor Tid', *Levende Musik, op. cit.,* 20; *Living Music, op. cit.,* 20-21; *Carl Nielsen til sin Samtid,* 84.

12 *Man maa vise de overmætte, at et melodisk Terzspring bør betragtes som en Guds gave, en Kvart som en Oplevelse og en Kvint som den højeste Lykke.* 'Musikalske problemer', *Levende Musik, op. cit.,* 50; *Living Music, op. cit.,* 42; John Fellow (1999), *op. cit.,* 265.

an abundance of canonic passages from the master himself seemingly allows itself to be readily taken as a confirmation for a puristic Nielsen reception; his essay 'Words, Music and Programme Music' of 1909, not least, has been a gold-mine. Here we may read, amongst other things:

> If you ask a composer what he meant by a particular chord or a particular succession of notes, in reality he can only reply by playing or singing the passage in question; all other explanation is nonsense.[13]

I shall return to this article's value as a philosophical source-text and will confine myself here to the observation that declarations such as this are in open conflict with Nielsen's practice as a composer. He was notoriously unable to explain what he meant by his music – whether by a 'particular chord or succession of notes' or by an entire work – just by playing it (or by having it played; he was no high-flyer on the piano, and his talents as a conductor are controversial). Time and again he had to resort to paraphrases and images, which in many cases admittedly strike one by their musico-poetical aptness, but which also from time to time turn out in such a way that one is tempted to turn his words against him and say: that's nonsense. It should also be clear that if – again to use his own words – 'in reality' a composer can only explain the meaning of his music by music itself, then we're talking about an abstract, purely theoretical reality. And yet, there really had been a time when music had demanded neither explanations nor philosophical reflection, but was able to speak for itself.

The philosophising Nielsen's sense of real reality increased with the years. Writing to his Swedish colleague Ture Rangström in 1920, he sketched a vision based on quite a different realistic foundation :

> In my mind's eye I foresee a new kind of musical generation, which will draw from sources not like shady thieves with careful hands, but as open and dauntless artists, who consider everything that is and has been as their natural property.... We shall hear with our eyes, see with our ears, smell with our hands, think with our hearts, and feel with our brains.[14]

---

13 *Spørger man en Komponist, hvad han har ment med en eller anden bestemt Akkord eller Tonerække, kan han i Virkeligheden kun svare ved at spille eller synge det omhandlede Sted, al anden Forklaring er Nonsens.* 'Ord, Musik og Programmusik' in *Levende Musik, op. cit.,* 31; *Living Music, op. cit.,* 29; John Fellow (1999), *op. cit.,* 129.

14 *Jeg ser i Aanden, at der vil komme en ny Musikslægt, der øser af Kilderne, ikke som fordægtigeTyve med forsigtige Hænder, men som aabne og frejdige Kunstnere, der betragter alt hvad der er og har været som naturlig Ejendom. [...] Vi skal høre med Øjnene, se med Ørerne, lugte med Hænderne, tænke med Hjertet og føle med Hjernen.* Letter of 16.2.1890, Møller and Meyer, *op. cit.,* 189-190.

Leaving aside the doings of coming musical generations, he himself indeed drew all through his life openly and dauntlessly from whatever presented itself to him as Sources: 'everything that is and has been', not only within music itself or art as a whole, but in principle everything that presented itself to his senses, feelings, understanding and fantasy. 'We cannot hear without having ears', he wrote in a diary entry of 1 February 1926, 'but we don't therefore have to believe that it's our ears we hear with when we listen to a piece of music',[15] and it was certainly not only his ears he used when he composed a piece of music.

It was entirely founded in his predisposition as a personality, and it is characteristic, that precisely in his childhood memoirs he would take the question up in more detail. In the introductory chapter to *My Childhood* he set out thoughts, which, slightly reorganized, can be boiled down as follows:[16]

The common origin of all thought, science and art is *poetic experience*, a special form of mastering of reality, which in its eternal present changes mere sense-data (for example the sight of a flock of geese taking wing) into part of a visionary sense of connection and transforms passive perception into productive activity.[17] We were all born with the ability to experience the world in this manner, 'the poetic gift', but most of us by far have squandered it by the rigours of existence and the incomprehension of adults. The great 'poets, thinkers, scientists and artists' are merely the exceptions that prove the rule. Nielsen stressed the distinction between the ability for poetic experience – 'the divine gift of fantasy' – and mere conscientiousness:

15 *men vi må ikke derfor tro at det er Ørene vi hører med naar vi hører paa et Musikstykke.* Schousboe, *op. cit.*, 491.

16 *Min fynske Barndom*, Copenhagen 1927, 7-8; *My Childhood*, London n.d., 10-11.

17 Like most of his ideas, Nielsen's notion of 'poetic experience' as the common origin for both science and art was profoundly personal. Of course this does not exclude the possibility that he got onto that track via his friends and artistic colleagues, thhrough their acquaintance with the doctrines of the contemporary French philosopher Henri Bergson about intuition and *l'élan vital*, which at that time were all the rage in symbolist circles. Nielsen took his idea quite literally. For example, in his 'Meditations' he portrays an artist (himself, of course) impressing a building engineer with his intuitive knowledge about the best mixture of sand and cement for making concrete. Nor was he alone in this area; his friend Sophus Claussen in a theatre review had discussed 'the Hamlet-like oblique glance, that seems to come right up from the back of the brain', only later to learn that it had been discovered that the optic nerve was attached to the rearmost part of the brain (cf. the Preface to his collection of lyric poetry, *Heroica*, Copenhagen, 1925). Even so, it is safe to assume that neither of them would have put their trust in building construction or brain surgery that was based exclusively on intuition. They both knew that specialist ability and patient application were also necessary.

Maybe it will be objected that the poetic gift consists in the gift for presentation. But presentation is after all only working out, which must be a question of training, culture and education.[18]

In other words: 'the poetic gift', the gift for intensive and fructifying experience, is inborn and timeless; the gift for representation on the other hand is acquired, and both historically and socially determined. And what gives the thing represented (for example a work of art) its 'rightness' (as he called it) or authenticity (as many would probably call it nowadays) is not 'working out' for its own sake, but what this working out – in all its ties to its time and place – includes of poetic experience. From his childhood on he had loved hearing people make speeches, and this irrespective of their oratorical ability:

> What captivated me was something that as it were lay beneath the surface: the impulse that drove the words, the gestures, the play of facial expressions, the circulation if I can so put it, and the entire counterpoint of inner compulsion, of distress and joy, of tension and resolution.[19]

Nor was 'working out' Nielsen's strongest point as a composer. His sense of form was good, as Gade had already told him in 1883, but not ideal; there are questionable transitions and formal lopsidedness in his works that cannot all be excused by the maxim that there is no beauty without a certain oddity in proportions. And as for the quality of his instrumentation there is still no agreement to this day. He was not specially interested in the 'finish' of his works and in general only placed a low value on their appearance as works in the absolute sense: as fixed objects inviolable in their perfection; there are numerous examples of his almost irresponsible tolerance in respect of conductors' and pianists' liberties with his creations. Not that he in any way put up with bungling or dilletantism, either from himself or from others; the 'basic skeleton' naturally had to be sound. But no more than that – self-conscious artistry was not his thing. What counted was his music's 'rightness', and that never lay in the working out of his music but in its presentation of what 'as it were lay

---

18 *Man vil maaske indvende, at Digterevnen bestaar i Evnen til at fremstille. Men Fremstillingen er jo kun Udformningen, som maa være et Spørgsmaal om Opøvning, Kulturpaavirkning og Undervisning. Min fynske Barndom, 7-8; My Childhood, 11.*

19 *Det, som fængslede mig, var noget, der ligesom laa bag ved: det, der drev Ordene, Bevægelserne, Minespillet, Blodomløbet – kan man godt sige – og det hele Sammenspil af indre Trængsel, af Nød og Glæde, Spænding og Udløsning. Min fynske Barndom, 6; My Childhood, 9.*

beneath': the poetic experience. 'Experience! Yes, this word is the gateway to the whole world', he wrote in the extract from his memoirs quoted above. And he continued by talking about his excitement with life on our planet, with creatures great and small, with plants...

Experience was for Nielsen not only experience of the splendour of intervals and timbres. For him music was indissolubly bound up with a many-sided, 'poetic' possession of all reality — be it great or small — that came within his field of vision. As a 15-year-old bugler in the 16th battalion in Odense he had seen pictures in his mind's eye accompanying the four company bugle-calls; with the first, for example, the sun had just risen, and 'there was a rank of soldiers, waving their caps in greeting'.[20] On the largest scale there were the thoughts and visions that came to him during his work on the Fourth Symphony (1915-16). When he confided them to his Dutch friend and colleague Julius Röntgen, it was with wise reservations over the usefulness of 'ideas' and 'explanations'; but, he added,

> [...] there is still something in the fact that even an unclear thought or perception can be valuable for one's work; at any rate I cannot free myself from a series of notions during my time of production, and that's why I suppose it's not so absurd for me to talk about them.[21]

It was not absurd in the slightest. It was solid experience that lay behind his basic motto: that music is life. And if he had ever had the opportunity to formulate the reverse — that life is music — then the empirical foundation would have been precisely the same. When he experienced his environment 'poetically' (which he naturally did not always go around doing), that meant the same as experiencing it musically. Everything that reality added to his life, through his existence as a biological individual, formerly the son of a poor man of the soil, currently a citizen of society and the world, as husband and father, professional musician and composer, was something that he was ready and willing to experience as music, and that with his considerable competence and from an unceasing inner urge he strove to shape and present as musical works. It was not just hearing and compositional technique that were involved here, but everything that he understood by Life.

---

20 *og der var en Række Soldater, der hilste og svingede med Huen. Min fynske Barndom,* 131; *My Childhood,* 111.

21 *der er nu alligevel noget om, at selv en uklar Tanke eller Fornemmelse kan have Værdi for Ens Arbejde; ihvertfald kan jeg ikke frigøre mig fra en Række Forestillinger under min Produktionstid og det er vel derfor heller ikke saa absurd at jeg taler om det.* Letter of 4.5.1915, Møller & Meyer, *op. cit.,* 146.

Programme music

To reflect on things and to fashion valid opinions was for Nielsen a process full of inner and outer contradictions, inhibitions and risks of derailment. There is hardly any more striking example of this than his remarkably contradictory attitudes to programme music and its associated issues .

Nielsen was not the only one to realise that programme music had its problematic issues; these date from the emergence of instrumental music as an autonomous art at the end of the 1700s and was a recurring topic in the musical debates of his time. But problematic or not, programme music had long since taken hold in bourgeois musical life, both in the concert hall and in middle class homes with a piano – and in the consciousness of composers too. Or maybe rather in their subconscious: Nielsen, who can hardly be said to have been unacquainted with the problems of programme music, at any rate did nothing to avoid its forms.

In the 1890s he wrote little piano pieces, Op. 3 and Op. 11, which with suggestive titles such as *Folk Tune*, *Mignon*, *Elf Dance*, *Spinning Top*, *Jack-in-the-box* etc. aligned themselves with a well-established romantic-bourgeois tradition. His weightiest contribution to the genre was, however, a series of orchestral pieces, each in their own way representing that form of programme music which since Gade had been preferred by the Danish concert-going public, namely the 'classically' orientated concert overture and the single-movement orchestral piece formally related to it – by contrast with the 'New German' symphonic poem à la Franz Liszt or Richard Strauss. We are talking about such sterling pieces of work as *Helios* (1903), *Saga-Dream* (1907-08) and *Pan and Syrinx* (1917-18), all of them centrally placed in his output, and also *A Fantasy Journey to the Faeroes* (1927, a commissioned work). He also enriched the chamber music literature with a piece of programme music, the striking little *Serenata in vano* (1914).

But that's not all. His contemporaries, who were inclined to interpret all music as programme music, made no exception for Nielsen, and he laid himself open to it. As mentioned, he could hardly resist *telling* what he had meant by his music, whether by this or that passage or by the work as a whole. For example, the phlegmatic boy, who in the Second Symphony (*The Four Temperaments*, 1901-02) is disturbed by a barrel falling into the water from one of the boats in the harbour;[22] the man who having told a good story empties out his pipe at the end of the F major String Quartet's second version (1919);[23] another man – perhaps Jørgen Brønlund from Ludvig Mylius-Erichsen's ill-fated Greenland expedition in 1907? – who fights with his back against a mountain of ice at the end of the *Theme and Variations* (1917);[24] the

22 Torben Meyer & Frede Schandorf Petersen, *Carl Nielsen. Kunstneren og Mennesket*], Copenhagen, 1947-1948, vol.1, 189.
23 Ludvig Dolleris, *Carl Nielsen. En Musikografi* [Carl Nielsen. A Musicography], Odense 1949, 159.
24 Letter of 3.1.1921 to Julius Röntgen, Møller & Meyer, *op. cit.,* 197.

grotesque fun and games in the second movement of the Sixth Symphony (1925), 'a little nocturnal tale, told with purely musical means'[25] – all these are selected more or less at random. But what should one think of the Fourth Symphony, which has not only a title — *The Inextinguishable* — and a motto: 'Music is life, and like it, inextinguishable', but also a regular programme: 'Life is indomitable; things fight, wrestle, procreate and are consumed today as yesterday, tomorrow as today and everything returns' – but whose Preface was nevertheless intended as a kind of anti-programme: 'no programme, but a pointer towards music's own domain'?[26]

As regards the question of programme music, Nielsen was apparently like a priest confronting sin: he was 'mostly against'. But it remained a thorn in his flesh, and it plagued him. This may have been the fault of his puritanical friend Thomas Laub, for whom the history of music since early Beethoven had gone down the wrong track , and whose opinions he always took seriously. Presumably he had also read Hanslick, or at least knew his definition of music as *tönend bewegte Formen*, which cannot have failed to strike a chord with him . And the blame may lie with the fact that things had been done — and still were being done — in the name of programme music fully sanctioned by the public, but which with his musical instincts he could only perceive as gross offences against aesthetic integrity. All this certainly contributed to the fact that in the above-cited article of 1909 'Words, Music and Programme Music'[27] he addressed the topic in detail. His aim with this was undoubtedly a double one: in part to set the public on the right path, in part to keep track of his own understanding of the relationship between music and everything that was not music but that still had a way of getting mixed up with it.

He took the opportunity to say many a pointed word about the relationship of the arts to one another ('the one art cannot flourish at all without the other', but any attempt 'to express the nature of one art using the means of another'[28] is an absurdity), about words and vocal music ('the relationship is purely decorative ... but in the same

---

25 Dolleris, *op. cit.*, 285.
26 The Preface to *The Inextinguishable* was printed in the programme for the first performance in 1916; it was subsequently included in the study score in the slightly shortened version, in which it is cited in Meyer and Schandorf Petersen, *op. cit,*. 2, 115. From the facsimile of Nielsen's draft reproduced in the same place we gain a vivid impression of the trouble he took to get it in the right shape. He didn't even succeed. His pupil Knud Jeppesen recalled (orally) that Nielsen left the responsibility for the final wording to him, but – whether out of modesty or piety – he omitted to mention this in his memoirs of Nielsen in *Dansk Årbog for Musikforskning* IV (1964-65), 137ff.
27 *Levende Musik*, 24-43; *Living Music*, 24-37; John Fellow (1999), *op. cit.*, 125-136.
28 *Den ene Kunstart kan slet ikke trives uden den anden* [...]*, ved Hjælp af den ene Kunstarts Midler at udtrykke den andens Væsen. Levende Musik*, 28; *Living Music*, 26-27; John Fellow (1999), *op. cit.*, 127.

way as the sun's relationship to things, which it illuminates, colours, shines on and gives glory and also warms and gives life, so that everything possible comes to fruition'[29]) and in an entirely natural continuation thereof also about programme music. He also said a number of things that may have hit this or that target but not the bull's-eye; as mentioned above, the article must be understood as not merely an objective elucidation of a personal problem but also an attempt at setting an errant public back on track, and understandably enough Nielsen stooped here and there to arguments on the level of his target group. In particular his conclusion regarding programme music is a remarkably weak-kneed affair, however straightforward it may appear to be:

> So is there absolutely nothing at all in the programme idea, given that so many artists – including many gifted ones – have occupied themselves with it? Indeed there is, but only a very few know where to draw the line between mere fantasy and the genuinely possible. And what about in music? If one confines oneself to a short indication or title, then music can illuminate and accentuate things from many points of view and in many ways, just as we saw in its relationship to the word. Of course. But then the programme or title must in itself contain an aspect of feeling or movement, but never a motif of thought or of concrete plot.[30]

He can hardly have thought that this settled the question as he had posed it to himself. We can detect symptoms of unease: 'strictly speaking nothing is fixed', he writes in what follows, and 'the question of how far one can go in this respect is of course a matter of tact and taste'.[31] Yet if we take his own output as a witness as to how far he himself could go, then the question of his own tact and taste becomes really rather precarious. Here there was no question of restricting himself to brief indications or titles specifying aspects of feeling or movement; here there was also a place and a

---

29 *Forholdet er rent dekorativt [...] men paa samme Maade som Solens Forhold til Tingene, som den belyser og giver Farve, bestraaler og giver Glans og tillige varmer og giver Liv, saa alle Muligheder kommer til Udfoldelse. Levende Musik,* 32; *Living Music,* 29; John Fellow (1999), *op. cit.,* 129.

30 *Men er der da aldeles ikke noget i Program-Idéen, eftersom saa mange Kunstnere – og deriblandt saa mange begavede – har befattet sig dermed? Jo, men de færreste forstaar at drage den rette Grænselinie mellem Fantasteri og Mulighed. Nu i Musiken? Indskrænker man sig til en kort Antydning eller Titel, kan Musiken fra flere Sider og paa mange Maader belyse og fremhæve, ligesom vi saa det i dens Forhold til Ordet. Naturligvis. Men Programmet eller Titlen maa da i sig selv indeholde et Stemnings- eller Bevægelsesmotiv, men aldrig et Tanke- eller konkret Handlingsmotiv. Levende Musik,* 41; *Living Music,* 36; John Fellow (1999), *op. cit.,* 135.

31 *Strengt taget staar intet fast [...] Spørgsmaalet om, hvor vidt man kan gaa i denne Henseende, er naturligvis en Takt- og Smagssag. Levende Musik,* 41; *Living Music,* 36; John Fellow (1999), *op. cit.,* 135.

need for veritable programmes, which included motifs of both thought and plot. And objectively speaking: where is the actual dividing-line between title, motto ('short indication') and programme; between aspects of feeling and movement on the one had, and motifs of thought and plot on the other?

In the interests of polemic and pedagogy, Nielsen had put the question wrong, specifically as a question about how far something that lay outside music could be represented and recognised, expressed and understood through the medium of music, and if at all, then what and how. To this question there is no absolute universally valid answer — indeed 'strictly speaking nothing is fixed'! But answers of this kind were exactly what he always sought. His instruction of the musical public was no proper answer to what in actual fact was the real question: the relationship between music and everything that was not music but that still had a way of getting mixed up with it.

To *this* question he had in reality long ago found his answer. Not through reasoning, but by instinct; he was so to speak born with it, and from first to last he held it alive and active in his compositional practice as an inner truth, in itself quite unproblematic, which with the years revealed itself more and more to his consciousness, without his at any point in time feeling obliged to articulate it in a completely thought-out and rounded-off verbal form. A reconstruction might look something like the following: Music is by its nature involved in everything that falls under the heading of Life, and a composer may therefore depict or express anything at all – on one condition: that it is inscribed through poetic experience.

If this condition was met, then for his own part all anxieties disappeared concerning words, music and programme music, recognisability and comprehensibility; Music and Life had once again turned out to be one and the same.

Translated by David Fanning

A B S T R A C T

Carl Nielsen's youth covered a period when art was no longer an integrated part of daily life but rather a commodity functioning as a kind of status-symbol. The article discusses Nielsen's attitude to this new situation, stressing the fact that for him art was still a compelling necessity, as expressed in his famous *dictum* prefacing the Fourth Symphony: "Music is life". With reference to Nielsen's own writings the article re-assesses his somewhat controversial attitude to programme music and the "meaning" of music.

DANISHNESS IN NIELSEN'S *FOLKELIGE* SONGS *

By Karen Vestergård and Ida-Marie Vorre

Carl Nielsen's songs have often been viewed as 'authentically Danish', both in Denmark and elsewhere. This perception seems to have taken root both with the man in the street and in specialist music circles. But are there any stylistic features that may be characterised as genuinely Danish, in the sense of concrete, demonstrable musical phenomena? Or is it rather a question of a construction, such that the Danish element must be considered an 'aesthetic fact', which exists in the consciousness of the population? [1]

If we consider the perception of Danishness in relation to music from a historical point of view, it is clear that the Danish ballads have played a decisive role in its definition. This is due to the fact that in connection with the flowering of nationalism in the 19th century it was assumed that the peasantry, which was designated 'the People', was uninfluenced by the international elite culture, and that it had therefore 'preserved' unaltered throughout history the original Danish essence – the Spirit of the People (*folkeånden*)[2] – in its character, language, history and culture. It followed that the genuine, unspoiled, Danish Spirit of the People was to be found in the ballads, viewed as the People's very own art-form, which – by contrast with art

---

* In this article 'folkelig' and 'folkelighed', literally 'folklike' and 'folklikeness' have been left untranslated. They connote both 'People' and 'Folk', but are not adequately rendered by either 'popular' or 'folksy'. They imply something shared between broad social groupings, in particular the urban middle class and the rural population, rather than exclusive to the latter. In the second half of the article, 'Alsang', here translated as 'mass song' or 'mass singing', has nothing to do with the Soviet *massovaya pesnya*; it is a phenomenon peculiar to the period of the Nazi occupation in Denmark, when it was used as a formalized means of social cohesion through the singing of Danish songs, hinting at 'spiritual' opposition towards the occupying forces. [Editor's note]

1 Carl Dahlhaus makes use of this term in his discussion of music and nationalism. See Carl Dahlhaus, 'Nationalism and Music', *Between Romanticism and Modernism. Four Studies in the Music of the Later Nineteenth Century*, Los Angeles 1980, 79-100 and Carl Dahlhaus, *Nineteenth-Century Music*, Los Angeles 1989, 38.

2 This term, and the ideas associated with it, comes from Johann Gottfried Herder's thesis of the 1770s about *der Volksgeist*.

music – was free from the influence of the rest of Europe. The specifically Danish element was therefore sought, rediscovered and reanimated by means of studies of the life and culture of the peasantry, and in particular through collections and publications of ballads. Encouraged thereby, a national-romantic trend arose among Danish composers, who tried to capture Danishness musically, amongst other things by making the published folksongs the starting-point for their compositions (as in Gade's *Elverskud* (The Elf-King's Daughter), 1851-54).

From a purely factual point of view, however, there is nothing to support such an assumption: seen historically, Danish folksong divides into two broad categories: a secular tradition represented by folksongs from the Middle Ages, and a sacred tradition represented by Lutheran chorales. According to numerous commentators, both categories have origins in European genres, which in principle excludes the possibility that they can be definitely Danish in origin. This would already seem to negate the possibility of authentic Danish qualities in music, in the sense of facts directly demonstrable in the musical material.

Against this background, there would seem to be reason to identify the Danish aspect of Nielsen's songs as a form of construction within a national discourse, rather than as a musical essence. The decisive question therefore is: How are these ideas about the Danishness of the songs constructed? From our point of view the construction of nationality may arise on several distinct levels: in the composer's *intentions* with the songs, in their *practical use* for communal singing (*fællessang*), or in their published *reception*. The present article examines the above-mentioned possibilities[3] by taking as its starting point the 35 songs that make up Nielsen's contribution to the *Folk High School Songbook* (Folkehøjskolens Melodibog), 1993 edition. Since, as mentioned, we wanted partly to focus on the national constructions in connection with the use of the songs, Nielsen's contribution to this collection seems to offer a ready-made selection, in that this repertoire has for generations made up the core of the Danish communal song repertoire: the so-called 'Treasury of Danish Song' (*den danske sangskat*). By way of introduction we have considered it relevant to sketch certain principal trends in nationally-orientated *folkelig* communal singing among ordinary people, from Nikolaj Frederik Severin Grundtvig's[4] ideas about folk-enlightenment, Folk High Schools, and communal singing through

---

3 See Karen Vestergård & Ida-Marie Vorre, *Den danske Sang – en undersøgelse af danskheden i Carl Nielsens sange* [The Danish Song – an investigation of the Danishness of Carl Nielsen's Songs], (dissertation, University of Aalborg 2006), which gives further arguments for and elaboration of the position outlined here.

4 Danish historian, poet, politician and educator (1783-1872).

the growth of communal singing in High Schools in the second half of the 19th century, to the use of communal singing up to the present day, a period when communal singing and the growth of nationalism among the broad population in Denmark may to a great extent be said to have gone hand in hand.

The History of *folkelig* Communal Singing

Grundtvig formulated his ideas for the Folk High School in 1832. His aim with this institution was that the rural population, which Grundtvig thought had retained 'the Danish Spirit of the People' most genuinely, should be awakened to an awareness of being Danish, through information about the homeland, Danish history, Nordic mythology, Christianity and the cultural heritage. For him 'the People' were identical with Danes (especially farmers) just as 'Danishness' in many ways meant the same thing as – or had a dialectic relationship to *folkelighed*. The latter term is a key word in Grundtvig's ideas on education, and the significance of this for him was many-sided. It meant both the specific qualities in the Danish people and the fact that there should be social equality in the nation; the goal he strove for with popular education at the High Schools was in the first place to promote a self-aware Folk Culture, which did not seek to disseminate the ruling class's cosmopolitan culture to the whole of society, but on the contrary had its point of departure in the People's own preoccupations and experiences. Folk Culture in Grundtvig's eyes would therefore be an authentic Danish culture, in that it would be rooted in the way of life of the country folk and at the same time safeguard a genuine Danish culture and maintain old Danish traditions (or what was seen as such). Grundtvig's aims with the Folk High Schools were, however, first and foremost political, in that the intention was to safeguard Denmark from German political influence. 'The People', so Grundtvig thought, were an essential and resource-rich part of society, which through education could be aroused to take part in political life in Denmark, make it more Danish and secure Denmark's future existence. The slumbering Spirit of the People should therefore be woken to consciousness with the High School pupils, so that they would come to feel themselves as part of a historical and *folkelig* community, thus being able to 'experience' their own Danish identity. According to Grundtvig the means by which this could be realised were to teach about Denmark and 'Danish values' through lectures, discussions and not least communal singing in the mother tongue. Grundtvig himself wrote numerous song texts, which came to define a core-repertoire in community singing in the first High School generations. These were written in a consciously non-elite *folkelig* style, in that they presented history, with rural life as the frame of reference and with simple construction and easily comprehensible language. The philosophy behind this project was that once the individual pupils had been educated and awoken, as they presumably would be in this way at High School, then they would become aware of themselves as Danes and subsequently become politically engaged.

After Denmark ceded South Jutland to Germany in 1864, there arose a great need among the population to safeguard 'Danishness', and on the initiative of Grundtvig's adherents – the Grundtvigians – various Folk High Schools were founded in the countryside regions in the following years. The High Schools became tremendously popular with the countryside population and were to a high degree contributory to its gaining a new self-understanding and self-reliance. Many professed Grundtvig's outlook on life and his ideal of 'Folk Culture', and Grundtvigianism therefore came to a great extent to influence the farmers' life-style in their homes and in the many new societies, where people found common interests of political, professional, economic or social kinds. The tradition of communal singing, which emerged from the High Schools, was particularly suited to express the farmers' shared attitudes, experiences and values, in that the song texts placed the farmer as well as Danishness at the centre of every aspect of existence, and the tradition thus found a way of becoming a fixed element in the culture of the rural population. With this a tradition of communal song established itself, in which the song texts showed a clear focus on the national. Helped along the way by the institutional school song, through which a homogeneous culture, loyal to the State, should be fostered, 'patriotic songs' became an integral part of everyday life for most Danes, and many of these songs found dissemination across geographical and social layers.

The rapid growth of communal singing and the production of song texts for it in connection with the growth of Grundtvigianism, quickly produced a kind of melody famine. At the High Schools they used already available or often just arbitrarily selected melodies, which fitted the metre of the poems, irrespective of the suitability of those melodies for communal singing. However, the desire quickly emerged to establish a firm tradition of melodies, in which each song-text would have its own melody, and after several decades with more or less successful attempts to contribute to such a tradition, an intense debate emerged at the beginning of the 20th century concerning the musical style of the *folkelig* song. One result of this was the publication of a whole succession of *folkelige* collections of songs, e.g. Johan Borup's *Danish Songbook* (Dansk Sangbog) (1914 and 1916) and Nielsen and Thomas Laub's *A Score of Danish Songs* (En Snes danske Viser I-II), in two volumes (1915 and 1917). These collections aimed at a renewal of *folkelig* song, but the new thoughts – and notes – only made a significant breakthrough with the publication of the *Folk High School Songbook* in 1922. The editors of this publication were Nielsen, Thomas Laub, Oluf Ring and Thorvald Aagaard, and in the preface they set out their aims: to create a collection of melodies with the right '*folkelig* Danish character' to be used for Danish communal singing. At the same time they expressed the hope that the collection would be used in all settings where *folkelig* song was practised.[5] Their efforts are reflected in the fact that more than one third of the book's 600 melodies were newly composed (for the most part by the editors themselves).[6] At the same time as the musical renewal of the High Schools' communal song repertoire, this publication also brought about a change in the choice of song texts, based on the ideal both to preserve the heritage of song texts and at the same time to broaden awareness of a new generation of *folkelige* poets from various regions of the countryside, who described their native surroundings with pride.[7]

The *Folk High School Songbook* of 1922 was thus epoch-making both in relation to a broader literary line and in its supplying of an extensive number of new (would-be) *folkelige* melodies, which replaced the motley collection of melodies that had hitherto been used for popular communal singing. After the publication of this melody book, its songs came to constitute the core repertoire not only of High School singing but also of singing in the State Schools, and the seeds were thereby sown for a fusion of School singing and High School singing, which eventually produced what became known as 'the Treasury of Danish Song'.

During the German occupation of Denmark from 1940-45, the 'Treasury of Danish Song' – and especially its patriotic songs – experienced a colossal flowering. The country's continued existence as an independent nation appeared uncertain, which brought about an explosive rise in interest in everything that could be considered as Danish. National symbols (the King, the flag, and so on), the country's history and the cultural heritage, were all cultivated to a previously unheard-of degree, and in the first years of the occupation there were mass song gatherings (*alsangsstævner*), that is outdoor rallies with communal singing of patriotic songs. Mass singing functioned both as a 'spiritual rearmament' in protest against the German occupying forces and as a manifestation of Danish national identity. Nielsen's contribution to the Danish communal song repertoire featured prominently, and his songs were described as 'shining jewels in our treasure-chest of patriotic songs'.[8] And with that Nielsen's position as a symbol of genuine Danishness was manifested.

Communal singing maintained its status in the years immediately after the War, during which it more or less coasted. Gradually, however, a perception of nation-

---

5 Carl Nielsen, Thomas Laub, Oluf Ring, Thorvald Aagaard, *Folkehøjskolens Melodibog* (first edition) [The Melody Book of the Folk High Schools], Copenhagen 1922.

6 Not all these melodies were composed specifically for the *Folkehøjskolens Melodibog*, but the editors' contributions broadly speaking all came about from the effort to renew the *folkelige* song.

7 Frands Johan Ring, *Thorvald Aagaard. Mennesket – Musikeren* [Thorvald Aagaard. The Man and the Music], Odense 1955, 72.

8 Niels Friis, 'Vor store Komponist Carl Nielsen' [Carl Nielsen, our Great Composer], *Aalborg Stiftstidende* 6.6.1945.

alism began to spread at this time as something festering and politically loaded, which produced a distancing from patriotism and also from the nationally-orientated communal singing in the form and with the repertoire which had roots in the *Folk High School Songbook* (1922). Also the 'niceness' of the songs and their conformity with established society came under critical scrutiny in connection with the youth rebellion of the 1960s, which meant that the songs gradually acquired the status of a form of '*folkelig* high culture'. The consequence of this was that the traditional communal song repertoire was gradually partially replaced, so that popular songs, even quasi rock songs and foreign songs also made inroads into School and High School singing.

In some cases, however, especially since the beginning of the1990s, we can see a new cultivation of songs from the 'Treasury of Danish Song', which is either directly motivated by nationalistic impulses or else by a more 'unobtrusive', non-political interest in the songs. An example of the latter is a number of artists' CDs including repertoire from 'The Treasury of Danish Song'. The motivating factor here seems to be that the artists are seeking out the nation's musical roots – not represented by the ballads as it was the case in the 19th century – but by 'the Treasury of songs', which is now seen as part of the Danish cultural legacy.

Nielsen's Intentions

The first area we deal with in our search for clarification of the songs' status as specifically Danish, is to what extent Nielsen himself intended to give his *folkelig* songs a Danish character or sought to project any particularly Danish stylistic features. We look first at his own statements. Then we examine his choice of texts and the actual musical construction of the songs, including the interplay between text and music.

There is not much doubt that Nielsen considered that music may have a specifically Danish character. On several occasions he declared that between Danes there is a common, intuitive understanding of Danish music:

> With certain melodic inflections we Danes unavoidably think of the poems of, for example, Ingemann, Christian Winther or Drachmann, and we often seem to perceive the smell of Danish landscapes and rural images in our songs and music. But it is also clear that a foreigner, who knows neither our countryside, nor our painters, our poets, or our history in the same intimate way as we do ourselves, will be completely unable to grasp what it is that brings us to hear and tremble with sympathetic understanding.[9]

---

9 Carl Nielsen, 'Svensk Musikfest' [Swedish Music Festival], *Politiken* 14.6.1906, reproduced in John Fellow, *Carl Nielsen til sin samtid*, Copenhagen 1999, 88-89.

In other contexts Nielsen likewise stated that it was 'the spirit of Danish folksong' which triggered this 'trembling understanding' of the music – that the spirit and the notes were two sides of the same thing.[10] So the thread back to the 19th-century belief in the 'Spirit of the People' as an underlying power that manifests itself in art, seems to be clear: understanding of national art proceeds from a collective consciousness and takes place with the individual on an intuitive level. In the composer's description, therefore, Danishness in music seems to be a spontaneous 'spiritual' factor, which can best be described via the feelings it awakens, rather than as a set of musical characteristics that can be pointed out in the musical material.

While Nielsen thereby acknowledged and extolled a Danish quality in music, he nevertheless often expressed a strong aversion to consciously intended national music, as embodied in the work of national-romantic composers.[11] In this light Nielsen's attitude to Danishness in music seems broadly speaking to boil down to discriminating between *wanting to be* and purely and simply *being* Danish. In other words, Nielsen was against consciously intentional nationalism in art, while he felt he recognised a national element in Danish music as an unconscious drive in the composer's work and as a manifestation of Danish spirit and feeling. This is also confirmed by the following statement: 'I myself think that both in my personality and in my art I am Danish – fortunately.'[12]

Even though Nielsen thus seems to have been very clear about his relationship to 'national music', there are also signs that point to his understanding of the term *folkelighed* in many ways as conforming to the Grundtvigian definition of the term, which was most often viewed as being identical to 'Danishness'. This may be seen, for example, in the preface to the *Folk High School Songbook* (1922), where Nielsen and the other editors declare their efforts to give the new melodies a '*folkelig* Danish character'. Nielsen himself was not a self-confessed Grundtvigian, but both through his country upbringing and in his adult life he was in close contact with Grundtvigian milieus. On many occasions he expressed his sympathy and enthusiasm both for Grundtvigianism and for Grundtvig himself,[13] and his work on several songbooks for use in Grundtvigian circles, together with his numerous contributions to the High Schools' current periodical, *Højskolebladet*, themselves bear witness to the fact that he sympathised to some extent with the ideals of the High School movement.

---

10 See, for example, the official programme of the Open Air Theatre of 1915 and the article 'Dansk Musik' [Danish Music] in *Politiken* 14.11.1926, reproduced in Fellow, *op. cit.*, 188-189, 407.

11 See, for example, Fellow, *op. cit.*, 88-89, 354, 531.

12 *Berlingske Tidende* 30.10.1926, reproduced in Fellow, *op. cit.*, 404.

13 See, for example, Torben Schousboe (ed.), *Carl Nielsen. Dagbøger og brevveksling med Anne Marie Carl-Nielsen*, Copenhagen 1983, 458; Fellow, *op. cit.*, 201, 685.

In Nielsen's thoughts about 'the People's musical education', as they are expressed, for example, in connection with the publication of the *folkelig* songbooks already discussed, we can find several explicit similarities with Grundtvigian ideology of folk-enlightenment. Just as Grundtvig himself strove to write his poems in a simple, *folkelig* style, so that these would be easy to understand and remember, so it was also essential for Nielsen that the *folkelig* melody should not distract attention from the textual content. On the contrary, the music should support the text and further the aim of disseminating 'the songs and verses of the best Danish poets'.[14] This idea would seem to correspond to the Grundtvigian view of art: that *folkelig art* should have a high degree of practical applicability and should therefore be decidedly an art for use, which could further the project of enlightenment.

Nielsen's thoughts on People's education focused, however, not only on how the texts were to be disseminated, but also on improving people's musical taste:

> A lack of ability to differentiate between good and bad music is evident everywhere ... Couldn't we do something in the direction of folk-training in unison song around the country's meeting houses, under the direction of organists or musicians, who could draw attention to the quality of the melodies during the songs?[15]

In the same way as Grundtvigianism wished to foster national self-awareness in the People, based on its own premises, so Nielsen may be said with his point of departure in the People's own culture to have wanted to further its awareness both of Danish art and of the qualities therein.

Against this background it seems that in his view of his role as a composer of *folkelige* songs Nielsen was influenced by Grundtvigianism's very concrete ideas about *folkelige* art. He may therefore have been influenced by the rhetoric of Grundtvigianism around the terms Danishness and Folk Culture, when he composed his *folkelige* songs, and when in connection with the publication of the *Folk High School Songbook* (1922) he formulated the idea that the melodies should have a '*folkelig* Danish character'.

The *folkelige* activity was, however, not merely an ideological project for Nielsen; it was also motivated by his feeling of belonging to the peasantry. On several occasions he stated that by virtue of his rural upbringing he felt himself to belong to the People

---

14 See, for example, letter from Nielsen to Julius Röntgen, 5.4.1915 in Torben Meyer & Irmelin Eggert Møller (eds.), *Carl Nielsens Breve*, Copenhagen 1954, 146.
15 'Folkelig Musikopdragelse' [Music Education of the People], *Højskolebladet* 8.6.1917, reproduced in Fellow, *op. cit.*, 201.

and that he knew 'the thoughts and feelings of the ordinary man.'[16] That Nielsen felt himself to be rooted in the rural population also finds expression in his various accounts of how in connection with the composition of *folkelig* songs he felt himself to be a medium for what was best in the Danish people:

> It is remarkable that when I am writing these accessible, simple melodies, it is as though it isn't me at all who is composing; it is as though – how shall I put it? – it were the people from my youth over on Funen, or as though it was the Danish people who wanted to express something through me.[17]

Here there is an indication that it was the 'Spirit of the People' that virtually autonomously manifested itself in his music. But at the same time as Nielsen thought that 'the Spirit of the People' (which presumably had the same meaning for him as 'the spirit of the folksong') was influential on the composition of his music, he also had some definite ideas about musical construction, which may be said to represent a form of musical essentialism. In several contexts Nielsen argued for the need of music to go back to a more elemental and original form — different from 19th-century art music, which according to him was both overloaded and overbearing.[18]

The ideal of musical simplicity was one that Nielsen undoubtedly felt to be fulfilled in J.A.P. Schulz's compositional principles in his *Lieder im Volkston* from the end of the 18th century, which Nielsen himself pointed to as exemplary for his own *folkelige* compositions.[19] Schulz defined the *folkelige* song as simple, easily accessible and formed in such a way that the music served and supported the text,[20] and Nielsen's various articles and essays – from both before and after the publication of the *Folk High School Songbook* – make it clear both directly and indirectly that Schulz was an important point of reference. In this way Nielsen was at the same time keeping his distance from the 19th-century art-song tradition, which he considered had moved too far away from the 'original' in music.

16 Letter from Carl Nielsen to A.C. Meyer, 23.2.1918 in Meyer & Møller, *op. cit.*, 171-172.
17 Schousboe (1983), *op. cit.*, 456. See also Meyer & Møller, *op. cit.* 1954, 220.
18 See, for example, Meyer & Møller, *op. cit.*, 106 and Fellow, *op. cit.*, 262-272.
19 This may be seen, for example, in Nielsen's correspondence with Laub surrounding the creation of *En Snes danske Viser* [A Score of Danish Songs]. These letters are published in various sources, including Torben Schousboe, '"Det skulle være jævne viser": Notater om et skelsættende samarbejde mellem Carl Nielsen og Thomas Laub', ('"It should be simple songs": Notes on an epoch-making collaboration between Nielsen and Laub'), *Festskrift Henrik Glahn*, Copenhagen 1979, 151-182.
20 Johann Abraham Peter Schulz, preface in *Lieder im Volkston I* (2. edition), 1785. It should be added here that for Schulz the 'Volkston' did not have nationalist overtones but was exclusively a stylistic term.

Against this background it may seem at first blush paradoxical that Nielsen both perceived the Danish 'spirit of folksong' as essential to the nature of his *folkelige* songs and at the same time acknowledged the model of Schulz for his *folkelige* musical style, by pledging himself to keep stylistically within the framework of the latter's compositional principles. Our point is that Nielsen did not necessarily draw a sharp line between musical Danishness and the musical *folkelige* style. Nielsen thought that his songs, just as his other works, would be naturally 'Danish' by virtue of his own Danishness. By engaging with and placing himself at the service of what the Danish people wanted through him in his compositions, his music became still more Danish, but it also became thereby more *folkelig* in the sense that the ballads also were in the spirit of the Danish people. If in addition Nielsen strove in the compositions themselves for a 'primordial' simple style, his music would not only be well suited to educate the People, it would also correspond better to the musical principles that made themselves felt in the People's own songs — in ballads. In this way Nielsen's aims with his songs – with reference to Grundtvig's term of Folk Culture (*folkelighed*) – may be said to have been that he wished to create something that was not just Danish and folk-like (*folkelig*) but authentically 'like the Danish folk'. According to this principle his music would not be directly, intentionally national, but its *folkelighed* ('folklikeness' in all senses of the word) would – just as in Grundtvigian contexts — enter into a close relationship with Danishness, and thereby the songs may be said to be intentionally '*folkelig*-Danish' on a different level from the intentionally national music that Nielsen was reacting against.

Judging from Nielsen's own statements, his primary intention with the composition of his *folkelige* songs may thus be seen as folk-educational, not as an express attempt to give his songs Danish features. But in that one must presume that the reception of the *folkelige* element in Nielsen's songs was closely bound up with 'Danishness' – also in the purely musical respect – one can say that Nielsen had an indirect intention to promote a Danish quality in music, which was in the Spirit of the People. This did not – as it did with the national-romantic composers – arise from a distanced attitude to the People, but rather from the fact that he felt himself to be an integrated part of the Danish People.

Analysis of text, music and the relationship between them

With a view to assessing to what extent Nielsen attempted to give his songs the above-described '*folkelige* Danish character', we will in the following section give a survey of *folkelighed* in texts, music and their inter-relationship, confining ourselves to his songs in the 1993 edition of the *Folk High School Songbook*.

Nielsen himself named no criteria for the choice of poems for his *folkelige* song compositions other than that 'anything artificially literary' should be excluded. With this he himself indicated that the poems should be *folkelige* in the sense that we also find with Grundtvig: which is to say easily accessible, simple in construction and written in readily comprehensible language. At the same time it was decisive for Grundtvig that the poems should also be non-elitist in the sense that they took as their starting-point the environment and everyday life of the farming community, so that they could express common attitudes, experiences and values.

Viewed in relation to these criteria, it seems that this selection of song texts indeed has a high degree of 'folkelige qualities'. The above-mentioned environment is, with a few isolated exceptions, clearly rural and – so far as the rural community is concerned – domestic, and at the same time the starting-point is the Danish communal frame of reference as it was in Nielsen's day (and to some extent still is): Nature, the Christian faith, and the Homeland, together with general human feelings. The poems range over a broad spectrum in their thematic content, from carefree tales of situations and events, to more profound, philosophical, solemn reflections on existential matters, and thus they encompass various 'moods', at the same time as they illustrate many different aspects of life.

Also stylistically the texts appear to be *folkelige*, in that for the most part they are strophic, with relatively short verses, simple versification and a logical rhyme-scheme. Also contributory to their immediate usefulness and their degree of *folkelighed* is the fact that they are written in an easily comprehensible language, without complicated symbolism. In this respect it is also remarkable that they most often make use of the omniscient third-person narrative point of view, which gives the impression that the singer has been told the truth about the topics in question: a style feature that seems to be in step with Grundtvigian ideas about folk-enlightenment.

In order to be able to evaluate the composer's intentions through his choice of text, we have found it essential to investigate the degree of nationalism as well as the *folkelige* qualities in the original poems. Our analyses show that nearly a third of the texts in the songs here analysed are actual patriotic songs, with a nationalistic message as their main focus. These messages cover a wide range, from descriptions of inner, personal love for the homeland to motivational calls to appreciate and to be responsible for the country, both in terms of the national, historical awareness and of the duty to defend the country. Characteristic of these texts is the fact that they all concern love for the homeland, for the Danish 'folk-character' and way of life, for the Danish countryside and for the country itself, with its traditions and history. Taken together, these conditions make up the non-material values all Danes can in principle unite around across social and geographical circumstances, and therefore the emphasis placed on them in the song texts, combined with the omniscient narrator's point of view, appears to be an effective means for constructing and manifesting 'Danishness'. Apart from these explicitly patriotic songs, there are almost as many texts with nationality-constructing features though to a less developed extent. These conditions indicate that Nielsen found it important to spread a national message with his songs to a rather large extent and in accordance with Grundtvigian ideology.

Musical *folkelighed* seems on the face of it to have been a purely stylistic quality for Nielsen, which he rediscovered in Schulz's songs, and which enabled him to realise his folk-educational aims in his songs. But at the same time it appears, as we have described, that in all probability he also thought that his *folkelige* songs, thanks to their close connection to 'the spirit of the Danish people' would involuntarily acquire a strongly national stamp. 'The spirit of folksong', which Nielsen ostensibly felt manifested itself in this way in his music, seems impossible to pin down, but inasmuch as it was closely bound up with musical *folkelighed* in Nielsen's scheme of thinking, it nevertheless appears possible to investigate the extent to which he attempted to embody the above-discussed '*folkelig* Danish character' in his songs.

In Schulz's *folkelige* style, which Nielsen extolled, music assumes an accompanying role to the text, as already described, in which 'simplicity' and 'accessibility' are the key words when it comes to the musical construction.[21] Our analyses show that the songs we have focused on to a great extent observe the following criteria:

- They are strophic and in fixed metre, in either duple or triple time.
- They have a regular periodic phrase-structure with an even number of bars in each unit.
- The vocal melody is so far as possible syllabic; where melodic decorations occur, these are most often text-dependent, and there are no examples of actual melismas.
- The melodic structure is simple, and based on a diatonic mode .
- There is a marked use of stepwise movement and of melodies outlining a triad, most often laid out in arc-shaped phrases and sequences within a narrow pitch-range.
- The melodies are rhythmically simple and characterised by sequences and recurring motifs.
- The melodies are integrated into the accompaniment, which in this way has a supporting function.

---

21 Schulz's *folkelige* style is summarised in Per Drud Nielsen, *til månen* [to the Moon], Gylling 2003, 16-20, and our analytical method is based on this survey.

Yet especially in the area of harmony it appears that Nielsen in a number of cases may be said to have moved beyond the *folkelige* style. With Schulz a *folkelig* song unfolds generally in the major mode and remains within that framework. This falls in well with the fact that as many as 32 of the 35 Nielsen songs we analysed are in the major mode. However, it is also characteristic of a large proportion of the song-settings that Nielsen made extensive use of harmonic deviations within the mode. It may appear somewhat paradoxical that Nielsen often moved far away from the main key, since he himself declared that it was one of his compositional aims in this genre 'not to create interest by moving outside the key'.[22]

Our analyses also indicate that Nielsen sought a close interplay between text and music in his *folkelige* songs by paying great attention to the form, scansion and rhyme-scheme of his texts – that is the musical flow implicit in the text sources. In particular the rhythmic construction of the songs is often aligned with the poetic metre to such a degree that it seems to derive directly form it. It is more difficult, however, to give a theoretically founded demonstration of the extent to which Nielsen also succeeded in creating an interaction between text and music by translating the basic mood of the text into music, in that this aspect is bound up with a personal interpretation of the text. Nevertheless we venture the assertion that through his musical embodiment he was able to illustrate, for example, the differences in the rhetoric of his song texts. Against this background there seem to be reasons to conclude that one of the primary concerns for Nielsen in connection with the construction of his *folkelige* songs was to allow the music to reflect the poetic sources used, which applies both to their structural formation and to their basic moods, and which is clearly in line with Schulz's principles. By this means he made the songs easier for performers to pick up and thereby augmented their level of *folkelighed*.

The Songs used in connection with Communal Singing
Nationalism and the growth of the communal singing in Denmark's population at large can, as mentioned, to a great extent be said to have gone hand in hand, and the two phenomena have throughout history been mutually reinforcing: communal singing has been used to disseminate and manifest national messages, and on the other hand songs with nationally orientated song texts – patriotic songs – have to a great extent made it possible to create a solid tradition of communal singing in Denmark. This state of affairs has led us to suppose that there may be a relationship between the use of Nielsen's *folkelige* songs in connection with communal singing on the one hand and the reception of these songs as something peculiarly Danish on the other. On the basis

---

22 Interview in *Berlingske Tidende*, 9.9.1924, in connection with the publication of the new melodies for *Sangbogen Danmark*, reproduced in Fellow, *op. cit.*, 316.

of this approach we shall look more closely at the circumstances surrounding communal singing that may have contributed to the constituting of a national self-awareness – a national identity – in individual participants in communal singing, and further, whether the songs in question may have achieved a status as peculiarly Danish.

The basis for identifying oneself as Danish through communal singing – and perhaps along these lines for perceiving the sung melodies as Danish – may be sought already in the period before Nielsen composed his *folkelige* songs. In the numerous High Schools that sprang up in Denmark at the end of the 19th century, there were established (according to Grundtvig's precepts and in a goal-directed fashion) the experiences and the culture that were considered as furthering the formation of the pupils' national identity. All material and spiritual elements were permeated with constructions of Danishness, and at the same time the High Schools made available an interpretation of existence in which the borders between Danishness (*folkelighed*), the Spirit of the People and Christian faith were fluid, in that these three elements appeared as an inter-connected whole, as a single organism. Whereas the individual had hitherto had the meaning of life explained in church, he could now seek for himself answers to the great questions in life, such as his own place in the universe, through this organism-thinking, and in this way understand himself as Danish. Communal singing, which was understood as a fundamental element in this process, had the advantage that it enabled the pupils both to expand their knowledge of the homeland and its history and at the same time to strengthen their feeling of community through the physical and spiritual activity stemming from their singing together. A large proportion of the song texts used were by Grundtvig himself, in which statements about the homeland, the Spirit of the People, the life of the People, history and the Heroes of Old were very often communicated in a rhetoric that bore evidence of his own linking together of the Danish, the *folkelige* and Christian identity. In these texts Grundtvig had sought to accommodate the demands of folk-enlightenment by communicating messages in a *folkelig* style. When at the same time he allowed the reflections or stories of his poems to take as their starting-point the everyday life of farmers (the High School pupils) thus using them as frames of reference for the poems, it is highly probable that the High School pupils would have been able to understand the song texts immediately and to relate them to their own lives. Through the simultaneous articulation of the singing group, the song texts could therefore immediately acquire the status of being an expression of communal experiences and values. At the same time it may be said of the individual participants that, by literally having the nationalistic words and feelings placed in their mouths as their own statements they could be aroused to the consciousness of being part of a national community. If one was thus enabled through communal singing to 'experience' oneself as part of a whole, in which both spiritual life and physical environment called attention to 'Danishness', it would seem obvious that the song melodies too, irrespective of their suitability to accompany the respective text or to be used in communal singing as a whole, were perceived consciously or unconsciously as a part of this 'organism'. Of course it is hard to know whether in the experience of communal singing any distinction was made between text and melody, or whether one experienced the national feelings the songs could awaken as arising from the song as a unity. But in that the songs can be asserted to have been a contributory factor in the individual's understanding of himself, through which national self-awareness was fostered, this would be in the form of a 'mirroring effect' whereby national feelings were projected back onto the songs (both text and melody), such that these feelings were experienced as 'Danish'.[23] Such a perception among 'the People', as would later be seen in connection with Nielsen's songs, can therefore on this basis be said to have been already present latently, even before he began to compose his *folkelige* melodies. Nielsen may therefore be said to have composed his songs at a historically opportune moment.

With the publication of *Folk High School Songbook* the musical repertoire was suited to the purpose of practicing communal singing, and Nielsen's contribution to this may to a great extent be said to further the communication of the messages of the texts: the simple, singable melodies lend themselves to the texts by reflecting their structural layout as well as their basic moods, the result being that there is nothing in the music that distracts the singers' attention from the message of the text. At the same time these texts – as Grundtvig's – to a great extent take their starting-point in the everyday life of the population in the countryside, so that the messages communicated – often nationalistic – were easy for this target group to relate to. Notable in relation to this context is also the extensive use of the omniscient third person, which gives the impression that the songs are communicating 'the truth'. These songs may therefore be considered especially well suited to disseminating or embodying national messages, and it is thus highly likely that the new melodies were instrumental in promoting national identity. In the same way, one may reasonably assert that the probability of understanding the musical side of these songs as especially Danish grows with this high degree of stylistic *folkelighed*.

Whereas Danish 19th-century nationalism was to a great extent motivated by a political demand for national self-reliance in relation to Germany, which at that time had political control over South Jutland, one can imagine that the need to manifest Danishness in the period after 1920 when Denmark recovered this territory,

---

23 These considerations apply similarly to the practice of communal singing in schools, and also in circles surrounding the national folk high schools where the Grundtvigian ideology – including nationalism – was circulating in the second half of the 19th century.

was of diminishing urgency. At the same time, however, it is conceivable that the new communal singing repertoire, which dates from the publication of the first edition of the *Folk High School Songbook* in 1922, and which 'set the tone' both for High School communal singing and for the official School song repertoire, contributed to the fostering of national identity and therefore to preserving nationalism.

In connection with the German occupation of Denmark during the Second World War, in which there was seen a new passionate interest in everything that was Danish, these songs – especially those contributed by Nielsen – received renewed attention, as stated above. With the aim of manifesting the individual's national feeling as well as a national group-identity, these songs were now sung at Mass Song rallies. With songs as prescriptions for feeling, and in settings which automatically had a great focus on 'Danishness', one could thus through a goal-directed process strengthen one's national feelings. If the melodies were in addition experienced as Danish, this may be connected with the fact that a kind of mirroring effect also took place here, such that the national feelings, which the texts directly induced, were projected back both onto the text and onto the melody, while both were perceived as embodying especially Danish qualities. Another decisive factor may be, moreover, that at this time and in the following years there was presumably a special willingness to assign those melodies that were part of furthering the feeling of Danish national identity a status as something especially Danish.

In the period from the Second World War until today, when the general attitude to nationalism has gradually become modified, and other frames of reference have come to dominate, 'Danish identity' has similarly changed from being received as some kind of inviolable truism to being viewed as an attitude that an individual may choose to adopt. At the same time the use of 'the Danish Song Treasury' seems to have narrowed to communal singing in traditional contexts, alongside a new song repertoire, in recent times having its musical qualities stressed or being used with a very clear political agenda. With the exception of the last-named case, the songs can therefore no longer be said to have the same degree of 'identity-forming effect' for the population at large as they previously had in the High Schools and at the time of the German Occupation, for which reason the chances of the younger generation's perceiving the songs as peculiarly Danish likewise seem less pronounced.

In more general terms there would nevertheless seem to be grounds for asserting that the perception in the broad population of Nielsen's songs as 'specifically Danish', in all probability arose from the population's own experiences with the practice outlined here of communal singing in those settings where Danishness was fostered. The textual content of the songs appears inevitably more 'trustworthy' in communal singing, in that they acquire the function of expressing a communal conviction, supported by the surrounding culture. If the song texts have still been able to awaken the national feelings of the individual singer, such that the singer has been able to experience himself as Danish – and as a part of a Danish community – then presumably a form of mirroring has taken place in the singer's consciousness, such that not only the textual but also the musical elements of the songs have been understood as sources of these feelings, whereby they are 'recognised' as Danish. Of course it is difficult to judge to what extent the individual participants in communal singing reflected on 'Danishness' in Nielsen's songs but there nevertheless seems to be a strong likelihood that the widespread use of the songs in settings where Danishness was a focus left its mark on their perception.

The Literary Reception of the Songs

With a view to investigating to what extent the literary reception may have influenced the understanding of Nielsen's songs as something especially Danish, we shall now attempt to identify when national constructions in the descriptions of Nielsen's songs may be said to have appeared, and furthermore within which kinds of discourse this national representation emerged, functioned and became established.[24] Our survey is based both on journalistic criticism of the songs in their own day and on musicological reception in the form of contemporary and later articles from journals and newspapers, together with biographies, in order to give us an impression of how far the attitudes represented by that reception were disseminated in specialist music circles alone, or whether they may also be presumed to have reached a broader sector of the population via journalism.

It is precisely journalistic contributions from Carl Nielsen's time that show that reviewers up to and including the publication of *A Score of Danish Songs* (En Snes danske Viser) did not definitely assign national meaning to Nielsen's songs. According to Fie Thaning, the scepticism of critics may most often be ascribed to the fact that at the end of the 19th century and beginning of the 20th, it was national-romantic music and the romance-song that were seen as a musical expression of Danishness. Already at this time, however, we can also see among some reviewers a tendency to consider the most 'natural' and simple – and therefore *folkelig* – songs as the composer's most successful contributions to the genre.[25]

---

24 Many authors have dealt with questions of reception history in relation to Nielsen. One of the most recent dissertations is Fie Louise Skovsbøg Thaning, *Nationalitetskonstruktioner i receptionen af Carl Nielsen – en receptionshistorisk analyse* [Constructions of Nationalism in the Reception of Carl Nielsen – a Reception Historical Survey], (University of Copenhagen 2005). See this source for a more detailed survey of the historical lines in the general reception of Nielsen's musical production, including the songs.

25 Ludvig Dolleris, *Carl Nielsen. En musikografi* [Carl Nielsen – a Musicography], Odense 1949, 28-29, 37-38, 50; Torben Meyer & Frede Schandorf Petersen, *Carl Nielsen. Kunstneren og Mennesket*, Copenhagen 1947-48, vol. 1, 103; Thaning, *op. cit.*, 24-26, 45, 96.

The split in criticism between those for and against the value of Nielsen's songs in a national perspective, endures until about 1920. However, around this time there is a change in the perception of Nielsen's importance as a composer, and this leaves traces in musicological accounts of him and his music, not least in discussions of the songs. In her survey, Thaning argues that the first performance of the Fourth Symphony in 1916 was decisive in relation to the establishing of a national frame of understanding around Nielsen, and that a consensus emerged thereafter as to his status as a great Danish composer, which manifests itself in the fact that it is hard after this time to find texts – neither journalistic nor musicological – that take a critical stance either to the composer himself or to his music. In the reception of the songs this is seen in concrete terms in the fact that the authors begin to evaluate them positively in terms of Nielsen's critical distance from Romanticism, and that his personal style becomes synonymous with the national style.[26]

Especially in publications from the 1920s and 1930s, Nielsen's songs are presented as 'genuine folksongs', and a close connection is found between them and an authentic musical expression in the form of folk music and/or early religious music (Gregorian chant as well as vocal polyphony of the Middle Ages and Renaissance). The songs become valuable precisely by virtue of the fact that Nielsen dissociates himself from 19th-century ideals and in places looks back to what commentators consider as the roots of Danish music. High School teacher Thorvald Aagaard[27] is the first to point out the importance of Nielsen's upbringing in rural surroundings. Thanks to his childhood, Nielsen is presented as a person possessed of an unspoiled, inherent *folkelighed* and thereby also Danishness, and this quality – according to Aagaard – is transferred to the songs, which thereby become infused with the Spirit of the People. The notion of the influence of childhood on Nielsen and his songs thereafter becomes dominant in the reviews and other texts. These two notions continue to hold sway through the time of the German occupation up to the centenary of Nielsen's birth in 1965, when interest in the composer flourished. In line with the growing scepticism towards nationalism, however, the following period sees only a few contributions to musicological accounts of the songs; moreover the nationalistic rhetoric in these accounts no longer seems so pronounced. Around 1990, however, at the same time as a general renewed attention towards 'the national', several musicologists begin to show interest in presenting Nielsen and his songs in a national perspective.[28]

---

26 Thaning, *op. cit.*, 46, 53, 97.

27 See Thorvald Aagaard, 'Carl Nielsen og den folkelige sang' (Nielsen and the *folkelige* song), *Dansk Musiktidsskrift VII* (1932), 11-14.

28 As may be seen, the historical lines in the literary reception of the songs can to a great extent be seen in parallel with the historical lines around communal singing and the growth of nationalism in Denmark, which are sketched above in this article. However, Thaning reaches a similar historical division of the reception exclusively based on her analysis of the nationality-constructing literature on Nielsen (see Thaning, *op. cit.*).

The part of the literature dealing with constructions of nationality from this time may, according to Thaning, be divided generally speaking into two directions:[29] while some authors stick to the models of explanation that were established already in the 1920s, others attempt to mark out new paths. In this connection it does not seem to us relevant to examine more closely those authors who represent the more traditional line of presentation of Nielsen in this period, in that these do not specifically discuss the songs but rather Nielsen and his work in general. On the other hand it is worth naming Daniel Grimley and Jørgen I. Jensen, who both represent alternative national-constructing interpretations of Nielsen and his music.[30] Both maintain that it is possible to draw a direct line between musical character features – 'processes of elementalisation', horn fifths and flattened sevenths and 'the falling motif' respectively – and the Danish quality in Nielsen; and they argue on this basis that it is precisely by using these features that Nielsen concretely embodied 'Danishness' in his music.

In general terms our analysis of the literary reception shows that the songs are assigned great national value from the 1920s on. Whether one looks at journalistic criticism or at musicological accounts, it is a consistent feature that the authors primarily focus on and emphasize the *folkelige* part of the composer's song production. The reason for this is presumably to be found in the fact that the terms 'the People' and '*folkelighed*' are of key importance in the prevailing view of 'the Danish', and that the *folkelige* songs, which thanks to their stylistic qualities were and are suited precisely for use among 'the People', therefore seem to be well adapted to confirming understanding in national terms.

Within this frame of reference we can observe two fundamental notions: on the one hand the perception of a connection between Nielsen and authentic musical Danishness, and on the other hand the notion of the *folkelig* as an essence both in Nielsen himself and in his songs. Both these general notions are anchored in the view of art that lies behind ideas about the Spirit of the People, and they establish themselves in the literature in the form of myth-making around Nielsen's personality and music: by virtue of an inherent '*folkelig* authenticity', Nielsen is considered to have a direct connection to a primordial Danish music, and furthermore he possesses genuine Danish qualities, which render him and his songs the quintessence of Danishness.[31]

29 For a survey of reception after 1990 see Thaning, *op. cit.*, 81ff.
30 Daniel Grimley, 'Horn Calls and Flattened Sevenths: Nielsen and Danish Musical Style', Harry White & Michael Murphy (ed.), *Musical Constructions of Nationalism. Essays on the History and Ideology of European Musical Culture 1800-1945*, Cork 2001, 123-141; Jørgen I. Jensen, *Carl Nielsen – Danskeren* [Carl Nielsen – the Dane], Copenhagen 1991.
31 Roughly the same view, so far as the basic notions in the literary reception of Nielsen are concerned, may be found in Thaning, *op. cit.* She considers that these notions are concretised via three specific myths, which she calls 'the myth of originality', 'the myth of childhood' and 'the myth of kinship' (Thaning, *op. cit.*, 3, 94-95).

If Nielsen's *folkelige* songs have therefore to a great extent been understood from a national perspective, both in musicological writings and in reviews and articles in the non-specialist press, this picture has permeated both music-specialist circles and the population at large. On this basis it thus seems highly likely that the general perception of the songs as something especially Danish may have sprung from – and have spread through – their published reception.

Conclusion

From the above survey it may be seen that Nielsen's own intentions with his *folkelige* songs, their use in the practice of communal singing, and also their literary reception, may all have been contributory factors in the understanding of these songs as something especially Danish. At the same time it is a constant factor in these contexts that belief in the Spirit of the People has to a great extent worked as a 'covert agent' and has influenced the perception of the songs in all these respects. Therefore we cannot say that just one or the other circumstance constitutes an explanation of how the perception of Nielsen's songs as peculiarly Danish has been constructed. The explanation seems rather to be that the factors described above have all been in operation within the frame of understanding provided by belief in the Spirit of the People, and that they have therefore mutually influenced one another and together come to constitute this perception. Thus if a person experienced or declared himself as a national individual through the communal singing practice of Nielsen's songs, and further if he saw these songs discussed as something especially Danish in reviews, articles and other writings, it is obvious that the person in question would not doubt the songs' 'Danishness'; in the same way it is obvious that music commentators and researchers have to a certain degree written against the background both of the composer's statements and of their own experiences with the songs.

Also the view of Nielsen as a national icon, as was already seen in the reception around 1920, but which was seriously manifested in the population at large during the Second World War, may be assumed to have had decisive significance for Danes' relation to his songs as 'national jewels'. That Nielsen's *folkelige* songs are claimed to be Danish – above those of, for example, Aagaard and Rings, whose texts also have a high degree of nationality-constructing elements – must presumably be seen as a consequence of both Nielsen's rural upbringing and his success among both 'the People' and the bourgeoisie. As a child of what was considered the 'un-alienated' People in the countryside, and much helped along the way by his autobiography *Min fynske Barndom* (My Childhood), he was perceived as an authentic, unspoiled Dane, who aimed to create and propagate something great for Danes. It is likely that it is also in this respect that we can find an explanation for the fact that those of

Nielsen's *folkelige* songs that do not have a nationalistic textual content and therefore cannot be said to have played a direct role in the construction of national identity, have also been perceived as Danish. One can imagine that a kind of synergy-effect has arisen based on the perception of Nielsen as the quintessence of Danishness and the function of nationalistic songs in the practice of communal singing, such that the perception has spread out to embrace the entirety of Nielsen's *folkelige* song production, whereby 'Danishness' has become an indicator for the whole field.

On this basis one may assert that the construction of Danishness in Nielsen's songs covers a complex network of aesthetic judgments and historical circumstances. Via the notions for which belief in the Spirit of the People defined the framework, the composer could perceive himself as rooted in the People and thereby as Danish, which gave him cause to feel that in the composition of his *folkelig* songs he was only a medium for the wishes of 'the Danish People'. At the same time these songs were able to participate in the creation of national identity and thus to be experienced as Danish; and finally the literary reception of the songs was able both to activate and to reinforce the notion of Danishness in these songs; taken together, these factors in their interaction constituted a self-reinforcing process.

If the nationally orientated perception of the songs still clings on today, when nationalism to a great extent is seen as 'politically incorrect', and the songs are in addition receiving renewed attention as national jewels, this may be connected with the fact that that perception is especially tenacious; the songs have once and for all been adopted as being especially Danish, and this perception may thus be said to have won status as an aesthetic fact.

Translated by David Fanning

ABSTRACT

Nielsen's *folkelige* songs have been linked in many contexts with something especially Danish. In this article we deal with how this perception has arisen — from the composer's declared intentions, from the practice of communal singing, and from their literary reception.

As an introduction we sketch certain central lines in the history of *folkelig* communal singing. With a view to evaluating the composer's intentions we then outline the main points from our interpretations of Nielsen's own statements and our analyses of text, music and their interaction, using the selection of Nielsen's songs to be found in the *Folk High School Songbook* (1993). From this it is concluded that in his own way Nielsen may be said to have had the intention to give his *folkelige* songs a 'Danish' character.

From our analysis of the practice of communal singing that surrounded the songs, there appears to be a great likelihood that the nationalistic perception of these songs may have arisen by this means, and similarly we demonstrate in the analysis of the reception history, that the published treatment of the songs may additionally have had decisive significance.

The explanation for how the perception of Nielsen's *folkelige* songs as especially Danish has arisen is thus not to be found in any single one of the circumstances here considered. Rather it should be seen in the light of the national discourse, in which ideas about a national essence, the Spirit of the People, have been prominent. The composer himself, the communal singing practice in which the songs were used, and their reception, all seem to have worked within the framework of understanding provided by the idea of a 'Spirit of the People', and in this way these factors may be said to have mutually influenced one another and at the same time to have constructed the perception that Nielsen's *folkelige* songs are especially Danish.

CARL NIELSEN BIBLIOGRAPHY 2004-2007

By Kirsten Flensborg Petersen

The bibliographies published in *Carl Nielsen Studies* – including the following bibliography – are also to be found on the internet at www.kb.dk/da/kb/nb/mta/cnu/studies.html.

Anderson, Martin: 'Thomas Dausgaard: Conductor in a hurry', *Nordic Sounds* 4 (2003) pp. 9-13.

Austen, Jill: 'Behind 'The Mother'', *Flutist Quarterly – The Official Magazine of the National Flute Association* 30/4 (2005) pp. 46-48.

Benestad, Finn and Dag Schjelderup-Ebbe: 'To åndsbeslektede tonemestre: Johan Svendsen og Carl Nielsen' [Two spiritually related masters: Johan Svendsen and Carl Nielsen], in *Musikvidenskabelige Kompositioner: Festskrift til Niels Krabbe 1941 – 3. oktober – 2006*, Anne Ørbæk Jensen et al. (eds.), København 2006, pp. 425-436.

Brown, Peter: *The symphonic repertoire. Vol. 3. Part A, The European symphony from ca 1800 to ca 1930: Germany and the Nordic Countries*, Bloomington 2007, 1168 p.

Bubert, Dennis: 'Orchestral Excerpt Class', *ITA Journal* 31:4 (2003) pp. 20-22.

Carl Nielsen brevudgaven [The Letters of Carl Nielsen], John Fellow (ed.), København 2005-, volume 1, 1886-1897, København 2005, 571 p.

Carl Nielsen brevudgaven [The Letters of Carl Nielsen], John Fellow (ed.), København 2005-, volume 2, 1898-1905, København 2006, 598 p.

Carl Nielsen brevudgaven [The Letters of Carl Nielsen], John Fellow (ed.), København 2005-, volume 3, 1906-1910, København 2007, 589 p.

Carl Nielsens Barndomshjem 1956-2006: Jubilæumsskrift [Carl Nielsen's home 1956-2006: Jubilee publication], Nr. Lyndelse 2006, 16 p.

Chandler, Beth E.: *The 'Arcadian' flute: Late style in Carl Nielsen's works for flute*, diss., University of Cincinnati 2004, 168 p.

Christensen, Erik: 'Danish music: The transition from tradition to modernism', *Studies in Penderecki* 2 (2003) pp. 89-93.

Christensen, Mogens: *Kreativ værkintro-duktion – til 9 satser fra Carl Nielsens symfo-nier* [Creative introductions to nine move-ments of Carl Nielsen's symphonies], Ib Thorben Jensen and Jørgen Andresen (eds.), Herning 2005, 128 p. + 1 dvd-video (Dansk sang B-serien, B DVD 677).

Christiansen, Anne: 'Fokus på billedhug-geren Anne Marie Carl-Nielsens produk-tion' [Focus on the production of the sculptor Anne Marie Carl-Nielsen], *Fynske minder* (2006) pp. 53-63.

Christiansen, Christine: 'Maskarade make-over', *Musikeren* 11 (2006) pp. 12-14.

Fanning, David: 'Carl Nielsen under the influence: Some new sources for the first symphony', in *Musikvidenskabelige Kom-positioner: Festskrift til Niels Krabbe 1941 – 3. oktober – 2006*, Anne Ørbæk Jensen et al. (eds.), København 2006, pp. 437-455.

Fellow, John: 'Carl Nielsen: Mere end musik' [Carl Nielsen: More than music], *Fund og Forskning i Det Kongelige Biblioteks Samlinger* 43 (2004) pp. 395-403.

Fellow, John: 'De er sure, sagde ræven' [The grapes are sour], *Dansk Musiktidsskrift* 80/3 (2005-2006) pp. 118-119.

Fellow, John: 'Fædrelandssang med følger: Du Danske Mand i hundrede år' [A natio-nal song and its consequences: 'Du Dan-ske Mand' through 100 years], in *Musik-videnskabelige Kompositioner: Festskrift til*

Niels Krabbe 1941 – 3. oktober – 2006, Anne Ørbæk Jensen et al. (eds.), København 2006, pp. 457-477.

Fellow, John: 'Nielsen og Furtwängler', *Magasin fra Det Kongelige Bibliotek* 18/3 (2005) pp. 5-8.

Fellow, John: 'Søn af Carl Nielsen i Bogen-se' [Son of Carl Nielsen in Bogense], *Slet-ten* (2005) pp. 22-32.

Fellow, John: *Vil Herren ikke hilse på sin Slægt. Brudstykker af Carl Nielsens ungdoms-historie* [Wouldn't you like to greet your relatives, Sir? Aspects of Carl Nielsen's youth], København 2005, 142 p.

Fjeldsøe, Michael: [Review of] Carl Nielsen brevudgaven. Volume 1. 1886-1897, *Danish Yearbook of Musicology* 33 (2005) pp. 127-130.

Follett, Christopher: 'Inextinguishable Nielsen' [Review of] Carl Nielsen Studies 1, David Fanning, Daniel M. Grimley and Niels Krabbe (eds.), *Nordic Sounds* 1 (2005) p. 23.

Foltmann, Niels Bo and Lisbeth Ahlgren Jensen: 'Det Kongelige Bibliotek som ud-giver af den nationale kulturarv' [The Royal Library as editor of the national cultural heritage], in *Umisteligt. Festskrift til Erland Kolding Nielsen*, John T. Lau-ridsen and Olaf Olsen (eds.), København 2007, pp. 571-588.

Gangsted-Rasmussen, Niels: 'Fire højesteretssagførere og en forsinket rytter' [Four barristers and a late horseman], in *Musikvidenskabelige Kompositioner: Festskrift til Niels Krabbe 1941 – 3. oktober – 2006*, Anne Ørbæk Jensen et al. (eds.), København 2006, pp. 479-487.

Grimley, Daniel M.: 'Carl Nielsen's Historicist modernism: Gesture and identity in the Chaconne for piano', in *Musikvidenskabelige Kompositioner: Festskrift til Niels Krabbe 1941 – 3. oktober – 2006*, Anne Ørbæk Jensen et al. (eds.), København 2006, pp. 489-501.

Grimley, Daniel M.: 'Horn calls and flattened sevenths: Nielsen and Danish musical style', in *Musical constructions of nationalism: Essays on the history and ideology of European musical culture, 1800-1945*, Harry M. White and Michael Murphy (eds.), Cork 2001, pp. 123-141.

Grimley, Daniel: [Reviews of] Carl Nielsen, Aladdin, David Fanning (ed.), Carl Nielsen Edition I/8, Symphony No. 6, Thomas Michelsen (ed.), Carl Nielsen Edition II/6, *Music & Letters* 85/1 (2004) pp. 165-168.

Grimley, Daniel M.: 'Tonality, clarity, strength: Gesture, form, and Nordic identity in Carl Nielsen's piano music', *Music & Letters* 86/2 (2005) pp. 202-233.

Guldager, Anne: 'Fra muse til massøseformand' [From muse to chairman of the masseuses], *Fysioterapeuten* 87/12 (2005) pp. 22-26.

Hauge, Peter: 'Carl Nielsen and The Gothenburg Orchestral Society 1914-31: contact, programming, and repertoire', *Carl Nielsen Studies* 2 (2005) pp. 7-35.

Isaacson, Lanae H.: [Review of] Carl Nielsen til sin samtid [Nielsen to his contemporaries], John Fellow (ed.), *Scandinavian Studies* 72/2 (2000) pp. 244-246.

Isaacson, Lanae H.: [Review of] Jack Lawson: Carl Nielsen, *Scandinavian Studies* 70/2 (1998) pp. 284-286.

Isaacson, Lanae H.: [Review of] Jørgen I. Jensen, Carl Nielsen, the Dane – a musical biography, *Scandinavian Studies* 64/3 (1992) pp. 484-487.

Isaacson, Lanae H.: [Review of] Steen Chr. Steensen, Music is life: A biography of Carl Nielsen (Includes a 3-CD set, 'Carl Nielsen, De seks symfonier' performed by the London Symphony Orchestra under the direction of Ole Schmidt, 1973-74), *Scandinavian Studies* 74/2 (2002) pp. 249-251.

Jakobsen, Erik H. A.: [Review of] Carl Nielsen brevudgaven [The Letters of Carl Nielsen], Volume 1, 1886-1897, John Fellow (ed.); John Fellow, Vil Herren ikke hilse på sin slægt [Wouldn't you like to greet your relatives, Sir? Aspects of Carl Nielsen's youth]; Mogens Christensen, Kreativ værkintrodukion – til 9 satser fra Carl Nielsens symfonier [Creative introductions – to 9 movements from Nielsen's symphonies], *Dansk Musiktidsskrift* 80/1 (2005/2006) pp. 37-42.

Jakobsen, Erik H. A.: [Review of] Carl Nielsen Studies, Volume 1, *Dansk Musiktidsskrift* 79/3 (2004-2005) pp. 107-110.

Jakobsen, Erik H. A.: [Review of] Carl Nielsen Studies, Volume 2, *Dansk Musiktidsskrift* 80/2 (2005/2006) pp. 76-77.

Jakobsen, Erik H. A.: [Review of] Steen Chr. Steensen, Lyt til Carl Nielsen [Listen to Nielsen], *Dansk Musiktidsskrift* 79/3 (2004/2005) p. 109.

Jensen, Jørgen I.: 'Carl Nielsen: Det symfoniske som kulturens hemmelighed' [The symphonic element as the secret of culture], in Jørgen I. Jensen, *Mødepunkter, Teologi – kultur – musik*, København 2004, pp. 159-162. Reprint: Resonans, Oslo 1996.

Jensen, Jørgen I.: 'Carl Nielsens Saul og David: ambivalensen i den danske sjæl' [Carl Nielsen's Saul and David: the ambivalence of the Danish soul], in Jørgen I. Jensen, *Mødepunkter, Teologi – kultur – musik*, København 2004, pp. 125-128. Reprint: Programbuch der Salzburger Festspiele, 2000.

Jensen, Jørgen I.: 'Det danske som musik' [Danishness as music], in Jørgen I. Jensen, *Mødepunkter, Teologi – kultur – musik*,

København 2004, pp. 27-32. Reprint: Klassisk musik, København 2003.

Jensen, Jørgen I.: 'Liv og værk. Om musikbiografi' [Life and work. About music biography] in *Liv, verk, tid – till biografiskrivandets renässans*, Stockholm 1995, pp. 3-11. (Kungliga Musikaliska akademiens skriftserie; 82).

Jensen, Jørgen I.: 'Music as art and science: An old tradition and two Danish composers, Per Nørgård and Carl Nielsen', in *Aspects of Secularization: Science and the Arts,* Søren Baggesen (ed.), Odense 1996, pp. 113-125.

Jensen, Jørgen I.: 'Musik som kunst og videnskab: en gammel tradition og to danske komponister: Carl Nielsen og Per Nørgård' [Music as art and science: and old tradition and two Danish composers], in Jørgen I. Jensen, *Mødepunkter, Teologi – kultur – musik*, København 2004, pp. 712-723. Reprint in Danish: Aspects of Secularization, 1996.

Jensen, Jørgen I.: 'Musikalsk og teologisk sprog i gudstjenesten: Notater om at diskutere salmemelodier' [Musical and theological language in the divine service. On discussing hymn tunes], in Jørgen I. Jensen, *Mødepunkter, Teologi – kultur – musik*, København 2004, pp. 66-76. Reprint: Organistbladet, 1979.

Jensen, Jørgen I.: *Mødepunkter, Teologi – kultur – musik*[Meeting points: theology, culture, music], København 2004, 808 p.

Jensen, Jørgen I.: 'Rued Langgaard 100 år' [Rued Langgaard 100 years], in Jørgen I. Jensen, *Mødepunkter, Teologi – kultur – musik*, København 2004, pp. 531-548.

Jensen, Jørgen I.: 'Sanginspektørens desperate træk: allegoriske religionskrige i dansk musik' [The desperate move by the music inspector: allegorical religious wars in Danish music], in Jørgen I. Jensen, *Mødepunkter, Teologi – kultur – musik*, København 2004, pp. 163-173. Reprint: Grib tiden, 2001.

Jensen, Jørgen I.: 'Århundredskiftet og musikken' [The turn of the century and music], *Nordisk tidskrift för vetenskap, konst och industri* 71 (1995) pp. 1-13.

Jensen, Lisbeth Ahlgren: 'Carl Nielsen and Nancy Dalberg: Nancy Dalberg as Carl Nielsen's pupil, assistant and patron', *Carl Nielsen Studies* 2 (2005) pp. 36-59.

Jensen, Lisbeth Ahlgren: 'Rosenhoff-affæren' [The Rosenhoff affair], in *Musikvidenskabelige Kompositioner: Festskrift til Niels Krabbe 1941 – 3. oktober – 2006*, Anne Ørbæk Jensen et al. (eds.), København 2006, pp. 503-518.

Ketting, Knud: 'Carl Nielsen and the radio', *Carl Nielsen Studies* 2 (2005) pp. 60-88.

Ketting, Knud: 'Carl Nielsens københavnske kompositionsaftener: Et delstudie i komponistøkonomi og receptionshistorie' [Carl Nielsen's composition concerts in Copenhagen: A study in composers' economy and reception], in *Musikvidenskabelige Kompositioner: Festskrift til Niels Krabbe 1941 – 3. oktober – 2006*, Anne Ørbæk Jensen et al. (eds.), København 2006, pp. 519-535.

Kildemoes, Nana: 'Anne Marie Carl-Nielsen: Musikkens Genius – et hjertebarn. Tilblivelsen af mindeskulpturen for Carl Nielsen, som i dag er placeret på Grønningen i København' [The genius of music – a darling. The making of the memorial sculpture for Carl Nielsen, today situated at Grønningen in Copenhagen], *Fynske minder* (2007) pp. 203-217.

Krabbe, Niels: 'A Survey of the Written Reception of Carl Nielsen, 1931-2006', *Notes – Quarterly Journal of the Music Library Association* 64/1 (2007) pp. 43-56.

Krabbe, Niels: 'Den danske musikkanon – generelle overvejelser og bemærkninger til udvalgte værker' [The Danish musical canon – general reflections and comments on selected works], in *Umisteligt. Festskrift til Erland Kolding Nielsen*, John T. Lauridsen and Olaf Olsen (eds.), København 2007, pp. 695-718.

Krabbe, Niels: 'The reception of Gade, Hartmann and Nielsen: Three Danish classics, and the role of the scholarly edition', *Fontes Artis Musicae* 52/2 (2005) pp. 116-124.

Krabbe, Niels: 'Wahlverwandschaften: Musikalske relationer mellem Tyskland og

Danmark i perioden 1760-1914' [Elective affinities. Musical relations between Germany and Denmark in the period 1760-1914], *Magasin fra Det Kongelige Bibliotek* 17/3 (2004) pp. 41-49.

Krummacher, Friedhelm: 'Steps to the Modern: Carl Nielsen's string quartets', *Carl Nielsen Studies* 2 (2005) pp. 89-131.

Kube, Michael: [Review of Carl Nielsen Edition vols. I/1-3, I/8, II/1-6, II/7, II/9], *Die Musikforschung* 58/2 (2005) pp. 216-218.

Kube, Michael: [Review of] Carl Nielsen Studies 1, David Fanning, Daniel M. Grimley and Niels Krabbe (eds.), *Die Musikforschung* 57/4 (2004) pp. 418-419.

Lichtenhahn, Ernst: 'David im Musiktheater des 20. Jahrhunderts: Bemerkungen zu Werken von Carl Nielsen, Arthur Honegger, Kurt Weill und Darius Milhaud', in *König David: Biblische Schlüsselfigur und europäische Leitgestalt*, Walter Dietrich, Hubert Herkommer (eds.), 19. Kolloquium der Schweizerischen Akademie der Geistes- und Sozialwissenschaften, Gerzensee, 2000, Stuttgart 2003, pp. 731-757.

Mamontova, Natal'ja: 'Karl Nil'sen: Portret i avtoportret' [Carl Nielsen: A portrait and a self-portrait], *Muzykovedenie* 2 (2004) pp. 57-62.

Mamontova, Natal'ja: 'Poslednjaja simfonija Karla Nil'sena' [The last symphony of Carl Nielsen], in *Muzyka XX veka: Voprosy istorii, teorii, estetiki—Materialy naučnoj konferencii* [The music of the 20th century: History, theory, aesthetics — Proceedings of the scholarly conference], Valerija Stefanovna Cenova (ed.), Moskva 2005, pp. 55-63.

Marstal, Henrik: 'Carl Nielsen: vor store (danske) komponist' [Our great (Danish) composer], *Dansk Musiktidsskrift* 80/3 (2005/2006) pp. 88-91.

Marstal, Henrik: *Nielsen: bliv klogere på livet med Carl Nielsen* [Nielsen: learn about life with Carl Nielsen], København 2006, 56 p.

Martner, Knud: 'Det sku' vær' så godt, Carl Nielsens Breve i inkonsekvent, fejl- og mangelfuld redaktion' [We had expected more. Carl Nielsen's letters, edited inconsistently and full of errors], [Review of] Carl Nielsen brevudgaven, volume 1, 1886-1897, John Fellow (ed.), *Dansk Musiktidsskrift* 2 (2005-2006) pp. 82-84.

Nielsen, Svend Hvidtfelt: 'Eksempler på struktureringer i Kurtágs musik' [Examples of structuralizations in Kurtág's music], *Musik og Forskning* 29 (2004) pp. 15-23.

Nil'sen, Karl: *Zhivaia muzyka*, St. Petersburg 2005, 124 p. [tr. of *Levende musik*].

Nordic Music Editions: symposium 1-2 September 2005: organized by the Niels W. Gade Edi-

tion and the Carl Nielsen Edition [at] the Black Diamond of the Royal Library, Copenhagen: proceedings, Niels Krabbe (ed.), København 2006, 105 p.

Oelmann, Klaus Henning: 'Zu Tradition und Rezeption des Streichquartettes im Skandinavien des 19. Jahrhunderts', Die Tonkunst: Das monatliche Online-Magazin für klassische Musik 2/11 (2004) p. 17.

Pade, Steen: 'Hvordan konstituerer kunststøtte kunstneren?' [How does art funding constitute the artist?], in Bent Lorentzen og hans musik: 27 artikler om klokker, operaer, sansning, planeter, æselspark, musikpædagogik, instrumentation, løvebrøl, opførelsespraksis, fyrværkeri og meget mere, Lene Lorentzen and Frede V. Nielsen (eds.), Hellerup 2005, pp. 179-188.

Pade, Steen: 'System og omverden i Carl Nielsens musik' [System and environment in Carl Nielsen's music], in Musikvidenskabelige Kompositioner: Festskrift til Niels Krabbe 1941 – 3. oktober – 2006, Anne Ørbæk Jensen et al. (eds.), København 2006, pp. 537-559.

Palmer, P.: 'A symposium on Carl Nielsen held at the Birmingham Conservatoire', Tempo 219 (2002) p. 46.

Pankhurst, Thomas A.: Desiring Closure, Yearning for Freedom: A Semiotic Study of Tonality in Three Symphonies by Carl Nielsen, Ph. D. diss., University of Manchester 2004, xv, 336 p.

Pankhurst, Tom: "We never know where we'll end up': Nielsen's alternative endings to the Flute Concerto', Carl Nielsen Studies 2 (2005) pp. 132-151.

Petersen, Elly Bruunshuus: 'Carl Nielsen, Quartet for Two Violins, Viola, and Cello, Op. 5', Carl Nielsen Studies 2 (2005) pp. 152-195.

Petersen, Elly Bruunshuus: 'Carl Nielsen, Søvnen, opus 18: en musiktekst bliver til' [Carl Nielsen, Sleep, Opus 18: creating a text for music], Fund og forskning i Det Kongelige Biblioteks samlinger 43 (2004) pp. 405-422.

Petersen, Elly Bruunshuus: 'Censur på universitetet? Carl Nielsen og Niels Møllers 'Kantate til Universitetets Aarsfest 1908'' [Censorship at the university? Carl Nielsen's and Niels Møller's 'Cantata for the Annual Festival of the University, 1908'], in Musikvidenskabelige Kompositioner: Festskrift til Niels Krabbe 1941 – 3. oktober – 2006, Anne Ørbæk Jensen et al. (eds.), København 2006, pp. 561-577.

Petersen, Kirsten Flensborg: 'Carl Nielsen bibliography 1996-2003', Carl Nielsen Studies 2 (2005) pp. 234-248.

Petersen, Kirsten Flensborg: 'Carl Nielsen's Flute Concerto: form and revision of the ending', Carl Nielsen Studies 2 (2005) pp. 196-225.

Petersen, Kirsten Flensborg: ' "Danmark, i tusind Aar" – sangens tekst, tilblivelse og reception' [The text, the origins and the reception of the song 'Danmark i tusind Aar'], in *Umisteligt. Festskrift til Erland Kolding Nielsen*, John T. Lauridsen and Olaf Olsen (eds.), København 2007, pp. 283-298.

Petersen, Kirsten Flensborg: 'Når "Aarbøger for Nordisk Oldkyndighed" bliver en kilde til Carl Nielsen Udgaven: Om veje og vildveje i udarbejdelse af forord til kritisk-videnskabelige udgivelser' [When Aarbøger for Nordisk Oldkyndighed become a source for the Carl Nielsen Edition: Tracks and wrong tracks when working with prefaces for philological music editions], in *Musikvidenskabelige Kompositioner: Festskrift til Niels Krabbe 1941 – 3. oktober – 2006*, Anne Ørbæk Jensen et al. (eds.), København 2006, pp. 579-590.

Ravnkilde, Svend: 'Altfavnende enere, sammen trods afstand: J.F. Willumsen, Carl Nielsen, Rued Langgaard – dansk billedkunst og musik i Paris i Juli måned' [All-embracing individualists, together in spite of the distance: J.F. Willumsen, Carl Nielsen, Rued Langgaard – Danish visual art and music in Paris in July], *Dansk Musiktidsskrift* 81/1 (2006/2007) pp. 26-27.

Røllum-Larsen, Claus: 'Louis Glass og Carl Nielsen: Modsætninger i dansk musik – Deres forhold belyst hovedsagelig gennem breve fra Louis Glass' [Louis Glass and Carl Nielsen: Dichotomies in Danish music mainly shown by letters from Louis Glass], in *Musikvidenskabelige Kompositioner: Festskrift til Niels Krabbe 1941 – 3. oktober – 2006*,
Anne Ørbæk Jensen et al. (eds.), København 2006, pp. 591-602.

Røllum-Larsen, Claus: 'Skovstemninger og stærkt sollys' [The atmosphere of a forest and strong sunlight], in *Drømmetid: Fortællinger fra Det Sjælelige Gennembruds København*, Henrik Wivel (ed.), København 2004, pp. 78-87.

Samson, Jim: 'Music and nationalism: Five historic moments' in *Musikvidenskabelige Kompositioner: Festskrift til Niels Krabbe 1941 – 3. oktober – 2006*, Anne Ørbæk Jensen et al. (eds.), København 2006, pp. 197-210.

Scavenius, Bente: 'Min bedste ven: et inspirerende venskab mellem maleren J.F. Willumsen og komponisten Carl Nielsen' [My best friend: an inspiring friendship between the painter J.F. Willumsen and the composer Carl Nielsen], *Fønix* 28/3-4 (2004) pp. 89-95.

Schou, Søren: 'Både Gustav Mahler og Carl Nielsen. Dirigenten Jascha Horenstein' [Both Gustav Mahler and Carl Nielsen. The conductor Jascha Horenstein], in *Et opmærksomt blik. Litteratur, sprog og historie hen over grænserne. Festskrift til Per Øhrgaard*, Christoph Bartmann et al. (eds.), København 2004, pp. 269-284.

Schubert, Giselher: [Review of] Carl Nielsen, Symphony no. 2, Niels Bo Foltmann (ed.), Carl Nielsen, Symphony no. 5, Michael Fjeldsøe (ed.), *Dansk Årbog for Musikforskning* 26 (1998) pp. 107-109.

Steensen, Steen Chr.: *Lyt til Carl Nielsen: symfonier, koncerter og anden orkestermusik* [Listen to Carl Nielsen: symphonies, concertos and other orchestral works], København 2004, 84 p. (Gyldendal Oplevelsesboks nr. 118).

Sørensen, Flemming: 'Anton Berntsen og Carl Nielsen', *Vejle amts årbog* 2005, pp. 17-20.

Thaning, Fie Louise Skovsbøg: *Nationalitetskonstruktioner i receptionen af Carl Nielsen – en receptionshistorisk analyse* [Constructions of nationalism in Carl Nielsen reception – a reception-history analysis], diss., Københavns Universitet 2005, 109 p.

Van Boer, Bertil: [Review of] Carl Nielsen til sin samtid [Nielsen to his contemporaries], John Fellow (ed.), *Scandinavian Studies* 72 (2000) pp. 356-359.

Vestergård, Karen og Ida-Marie Vorre: 'Danskheden i Carl Nielsens sange' [Danishness in Carl Nielsen's songs], *Musikbib* 3 (2005) pp. 4-7.

Vorre, Ida-Marie: "Som en mild og stille sommerregn...': om Carl Nielsens bogsamling og hvad man kan lære deraf' ['As a mild and quiet summer's rain...': about Nielsen's collection of books and what one can learn from it], *Fynske minder* (2007) pp. 169-181.

Vorre, Ida-Marie: 'To gange fødselsdag – to gange violin' [Birthday twice – violin twice], *Fynske minder* (2006) pp. 67-78.

Vorre, Ida-Marie and Karen Vestergård: *Den danske sang: en undersøgelse af danskheden i Carl Nielsens sange* [The Danish song: a study of Danishness in Carl Nielsen's songs], diss., Aalborg Universitet 2005, 154 p.

Wigh-Poulsen, Henrik: *Vær mig nær: Jakobs Knudsens skilsmisse og nye ægteskab: Beretning fra et Danmark i opbrud* [Be near to me: Jacob Knudsen's divorce and new marriage. A story from a Denmark under transformation], København 2005, 301 p.

Østergaard, Katrine Hertz: [Review of] Emilie Demant Hatt: Foraarsbølger [Torrents of spring], *Musikeren* 1 (2003) pp. 24-25.

Åhlén, Carl-Gunnar: "Ett geni av högsta rangen' eller 'Världens sämsta dirigent': Carl Nielsen enligt Tor Mann' ['A first-rate genius' or 'The worst conductor in the world'. Carl Nielsen according to Thor Mann], in *Frispel: festskrift till Olle Edström*, Alf Björnberg (ed.), Göteborg 2005, pp. 140-161, (Skrifter från Institutionen för musikvetenskap, Göteborgs universitet, 1650-9285; 80).

R E V I E W

Carl Nielsen Brevudgaven: Bind 1, 1886-1897, Bind 2, 1898-1905, Bind 3, 1906-1910. Compiled, edited, and with introductions and notes by John Fellow. Copenhagen, Multivers, 2005, 2006, 2007. DKr 398 each.

Carl Nielsen Studies 1 carried a concise Report (p. 166) on the setting-up of the complete Carl Nielsen Letters Edition, and the appearance of volume 1 was noted in *Carl Nielsen Studies 2* (p.233). Now the first three volumes are published, running to 571, 598, 589 pages respectively, and taking us roughly to the mid-point of the composer's career. It is hard to think of any 20th-century composer who has been honoured with this kind of comprehensive project. In fact with this Letters Edition, on top of the soon-to-be-complete edition of the music and John Fellow's collected edition of Nielsen's writings (*Carl Nielsen til sin samtid: artikler, foredrag, interview, presseindlæg, værknoter og manuskripter 1891-1931,* Copenhagen, 1999), Nielsen has suddenly leap-frogged from somewhere near the back of the queue in terms of availability of source-material to somewhere near the front.

Given the 1954 selection of the composer's letters compiled by the composer's daughter elder daughter Irmelin

Eggert Møller and his biographer Torben Meyer, and Torben Schousboe's two-volume 1983 edition of Nielsen's diaries and correspondence with his wife, supplemented by several smaller collections of his exchanges with various individuals, it might be thought that we already had a fairly adequate picture of his day-to-day life and artistic concerns. But no one who has looked carefully at the *Carl Nielsen Edition* could possibly agree, since each of the Prefaces in those volumes includes fascinating snippets of information from previously unpublished sources (in most cases using the good offices of the Letters Edition as it was being assembled). Moreover, anyone who places the previously published collections of letters side-by-side with the new volumes will not long remain in doubt over the value of the new project. Schousboe made no secret of the fact that family wishes had led him to withhold several letters from publication, while many of those he did publish contain elisions (most of them scrupulously marked). Now that those missing letters and passages are restored, they prove to be full of revealing detail about Nielsen's personality, his family, and his friends. Indeed some of the letters now appearing for the first time are quite striking in their existential angst. That goes especially for the fraught year of 1905, when he resigned his post at the Royal Theatre, came to the brink of divorce, and was somehow composing the miraculous hymn to love and high spirits that is *Maskarade*. And even the restoration of tiny details, such as the endearments with which Nielsen signed letters to his wife, helps us to take the temperature of his emotional well-being at specific times.

So while enlarged reprints of the old partial editions might conceivably have been an option, it is to the enduring credit of all concerned that the idea of a comprehensive publication was retained. The efforts of individuals and institutions to make that happen are laid out in John Fellow's introduction to the first volume, where he also traces the broad lines of Nielsen's development as a verbal communicator, the state of his preserved correspondence, and its relation to existing scholarly studies. Some 3500 letters from the composer survive, along with 500 from his wife to him, and a further 8500 addressed either to him or to those close to him, of which 2000 are judged sufficiently pertinent to be included in the Edition. That leaves only the single envelope containing letters apparently of such a private nature that Eggert Møller (second husband of Irmelin) had them embargoed until 2026, plus of course any letters that may turn up in the future. Some letters to recipients as important as Thomas Laub ap-

pear not to have survived; what a shame when that deprives us of Nielsen's part in the exchange that included a lengthy epistle from Laub about strictness and freedom in the renaissance style (vol. 3, pp. 483-489). There are also some letters presumed burned, including correspondence with Marie Møller, the trained masseuse who was connected with the family as governess from 1897 and who became the proximate cause of Nielsen's most intense and enduring marital crisis from 1915 (the many letters that do survive between her and other members of the Nielsen family are among the many fascinating new threads in the volumes under review).

Also in John Fellow's editorial introductions are succinct summaries of the main events in the composer's life and of what the complete correspondence adds (or, frustratingly, does not add) to existing published knowledge about them. Fellow has already extracted some of the most startling personal revelations for separate publication; and who could blame him? So we already know, for instance, of the passionate relationship between the student Nielsen and the teenage niece of his Copenhagen foster-parents, set out in *Emilie Demant Hatt: Foraarsbølger* (Copenhagen 2002, reviewed in *CNS 1*, pp. 184-188); and the complex picture of his other youthful relationships and their issue is recorded in *Vil Herren ikke hilse på sin slægt* (Copenhagen 2005). These topics, and the various details included in the Complete Edition of works, now take their place in a chronological unfolding that is absorbing in itself and made all the more pleasurable by Fellow's discreet yet scrupulous editorial clarifications along the way. As in Schousboe's volumes, Nielsen's diary entries are interspersed with the letters.

Several new angles (new to me, at least) emerge from correspondence not directly involving Nielsen but pertaining to his adolescence and to the national identity of his music. For instance, his former teacher Orla Rosenhoff remarks in a letter of 3 March 1905 to one of Nielsen's pupils who was preparing a biographical article: 'Danish or Nordic (Gade, Hartmann) he has never been.'[1] Discuss!! Also new to me is the correspondence with Nielsen's mother, lasting until her death in January 1897, and with his brothers and sisters abroad. But the highlight of the first three volumes is surely the marital crisis of late 1904 and the first half of 1905, which here unfolds more fully and more dramatically than ever before. I defy anyone who cares for either Carl or Anne-Marie, as artists or human beings, to read her heartbreaking letter of 28 and 30 March 1905 with dry eyes. The passages from this letter that Schousboe felt compelled to omit, and the build-up of pressure over the previous months, combine to make this outpouring of emotion overwhelming. Even after the couple's reconciliation had edged them away from the threshold of divorce, dark suspicions of the presence of another woman surfaced, despite the composer's promise that he had not strayed (Nielsen to his wife on 15 June). Perhaps the full explanation lies in the still-embargoed letters. The whole drama of these months is the more intense for the fact that the post generally took four or five days to get between Denmark and Athens, where Anne Marie was working. That was a torture for them both at the time, but from the reader's point of view it is a huge contributory factor to the unfolding of the drama.

The opening-out of elisions elsewhere in the correspondence between husband and wife often concerns domestic matters, though even those may be interesting as indications of day-to-day pressures (Nielsen reminding his wife about their agreement not to smoke tobacco; she recommending leeches as a treatment for haemorrhoids – vol. 3, pp. 533-534). More seriously, Schousboe made numerous cuts to passages that might have shown darker sides of Nielsen's character: not only in respect of pre-marital frustrations and dalliances with the opposite sex (recorded in volume 1), but also references to professional enmity and existential despair, not least in the diary-entries. Touches of humour, too, are reinstated: among the diary entries that were omitted by Schousboe is one for 20 September 1890 from Dresden, where Nielsen underlays Brünnhilde's motif from *The Ring* with the words 'Oh, you have diarrhoea in your stomach' (vol. 1, p. 121).

---

1 *Dansk eller nordisk (Gade, Hartmann) har han aldrig været.*

In a minor way, there are welcome details about Nielsen as a teacher, including the kind of detailed observations he made on his pupils' work (see, for example, vol. 3, pp. 457-458, to the father of an aspiring composer regarding a modest sonatina, and on pp. 478-480 a quite severe pricking of pretensions addressed to the more experienced Knud Harder). Even more enticing are the rare glimpses of political views, such as the expression of rather decisive antipathy towards socialism, in a letter to Svend Godske-Nielsen of 27 July 1910 (vol. 3, pp. 529-530). Such snippets have to be handled with special care, of course, because they are likely to be coloured by the views of the recipient (Godske-Nielsen worked in the finance ministry, as well as being a sometime composition pupil of Nielsen's). But this topic is certainly one I hope to see picked up in subsequent volumes.

Any hopes of revelations about Nielsen's major works are, it should be said, largely unfulfilled. As Fellow himself notes (vol. 3, p. 20), it is natural that the commissioned and occasional works should be quite well documented in the composer's correspondence, whereas the conception and execution of his symphonies, for example, was rarely recorded verbally, and then mainly in programme notes, interviews and the like, after the fact. Even so, given what Nielsen did confide during the creation of The Inextinguishable, it is slightly galling to find little or nothing of a comparable nature about the first three symphonies.

That is my only slight disappointment with regard to content, and it is clearly no one's fault. Indeed it is hard to find any serious fault at all with such a meticulously prepared and executed project, though Danes may spot more typos in the text than I did (I noted fewer than one per 50 pages). The level of user-friendliness is generally extremely high. The layout feels well judged, not cramming too much information onto each page, and the large number of photographs brings to visual life almost all the important characters in encountered in the correspondence. Once in a blue moon identifications of individuals are not made at their first appearance (as for instance, the German translator of Maskarade, first mentioned in vol. 3, p. 72, but not identified until p. 88). Volume 1 is supplied with a separate index of letter-writers, names and Nielsen's works; but for volumes 2 and 3 the index of names is not included, so that tracing references to, say, Grieg or Strauss, is impossible. Presumably that will be rectified on completion of the project, but in the meantime sticky tabs or pencilled notes are the only recourse.

For the non-native reader, it might have been useful to have in addition a map of Denmark showing the various locations where Nielsen went on holiday and composed, and also a street-plan of Copenhagen, to indicate his various places of residence and the halls where his music was performed. And while Nielsen's own language is almost entirely clear and non-idiosyncratic to a non-Dane, his wife's is more given to colloquialism and abbreviations, as well as being more hastily written; the edition quite rightly retains her imprecise punctuation (her younger daughter Anne Marie ['Søs'] seems to have inherited her disdain for the full stop), but there were times reading those letters when I did find myself longing for the parallel English translation planned at the outset of the Edition.

That may be a dream too far. But for the moment it is simply a joy to hail the appearance of these handsomely presented volumes, which will stand as cornerstones of Nielsen research for the 21st century. Few editors would have the dedication, patience and staying-power, never mind the specialist scholarly qualifications, for this job. John Fellow has put his fellow-countrymen and Nielsen-followers all over the world deeply in his debt.

David Fanning

LIST OF CONTRIBUTORS

David Fanning, professor of Music at the University of Manchester. Author of books and articles on Nielsen and Shostakovich; also active as a pianist, journalist and broadcaster.
(*e-mail: David.fanning@manchester.ac.uk*).

John Fellow, author of a number of novels including *Vækst* (2003) and editor of the Carl Nielsen Letter Edition. Also editor of *Carl Nielsen til sin samtid* (Nielsen to his Contemporaries), 3 vols. 1999.
(*e-mail: jfl@kb.dk*).

Lisbeth Ahlgren Jensen, M.A. (magister artium) from Copenhagen University; research fellow and editor at the Carl Nielsen Edition. Research interests include gender studies and Danish music of the 19th and 20th centuries. Author of *Det kvindelige spillerum* (The female room for performance), 2007.
(*e-mail: laj@kb.dk*).

Finn Mathiassen, professor emeritus (University of Aarhus) and composer. Research areas include the early motet, Danish popular ballads, Niels W. Gade and Carl Nielsen. Mathiassen's main contribution to Nielsen scholarship is his book, *Livet, musiken og samfundet: en bog om Carl Nielsen* (Life, Music and Society: a Book about Carl Nielsen) from 1986.

Kirsten Flensborg Petersen, librarian and M.A of music (Copenhagen University). Editor at The Carl Nielsen Edition from 1997. Research interests include music theory and Nielsen as a composer and central figure of Danish musical life.
(*e-mail: kfp@kb.dk*).

Karen Vestergård, M.A. of music and cultural studies (University of Aalborg). Research assistent at SNYK (Secretariat for Contemporary Music). Co-author (with Ida-Marie Vorre) of MA thesis on Nielsen's songs.

Ida-Marie Vorre, M.A. of music (University of Aalborg). Since 2006 director of the Carl Nielsen Museum and the Carl Nielsen House. Research areas include Nielsen's life and work, especially his songs.
(*email: iv@odense.dk*).